Stock Market For Beginners

2 books in 1

A Complete Beginner's Guide for The Stock Market Investing in The Best Way Through Strategic Active and Passive Investing

By **Brian Scott Fitzgerald**

Published By **Fitzgerald Publishing Group**

Dedication

To my mother,

Your unwavering belief in me has been my anchor in the stormy seas of doubt.

You've gifted me the power of dreams and instilled the courage to transform them into reality.

Your willpower has been my guide, and your love is my strength.

My life and achievements are all a tribute to you and the confidence you've instilled in me.

How to Make Money Online: THE SERIES

I created a series of 12 (twelve) books on How to Make Money Online.

Feel free to read any of my books in the series, which can be found on my Author page on Amazon at:

You can visit this link or Scan this QR code to get access

https://www.amazon.com/author/brianscottfitzgerald.

Contents

Your Free Gift.

Thank you for your purchase; I'm offering my readers the FREE PDF version of ChatGPT Prompts.

To get almost instant access, go to this website.

https://go.fitzgeraldpublishing.com/opt-in-stock-bundle

Or use your phone to take a picture of this QR code, and it will take you to the Website for your Gift.

Inside the book, you will discover:

- **3000 Prompts** To help you make even more money online.
- **Save time:** You can search for new topics to create content on ChatGPT.
- **Expand knowledge:** Our Package of ChatGPT Prompts covers various topics, from science and technology to art and culture.

If you want to make even more money online, grab this free PDF.

Wait, that's not all; just for buying this book and getting the free PDF above, you can also earn another free Book.

You can use your phone to take a picture of this QR code.

Use the latest AI techniques to uncover online innovation's future. Take advantage! "Beyond ChatGPT and 50 New AI Tools: The Ultimate Guide to Discovering Cutting-Edge AI Tools Beyond ChatGPT" offers endless possibilities. Explore a variety of cutting-edge AI solutions to transform your work. Discover advanced AI tools beyond ChatGPT on this thrilling voyage.

Grab this free book if you want to make even more money online.

BOOK #1

Active Stock Investing for Beginners

A Comprehensive Guide to Stock Market Investing and Trading, Unlocking Financial Success in The Best Way Through Strategic Active Investing

Introduction

Congratulations on picking up this, my first of two Stock Market investing books. Thank you for supporting your time reviewing this material I've delicately, thoughtfully, and meticulously put together to help you resolve two significant problems. The first problem this book will solve for you is eliminating the information overload and a sense of overwhelm many new investors face. We've all been there. Way too much-contradicting information is being shoved down our throats at every turn. We want to invest, and we want some guidance to help make the process more transparent, but there is only a simplified solution now.

The second problem this book is designed to help you is to give you all the essentials you need, without the fluff and hype, so that you can build a strong investing foundation that enables you to start small and grow into your empire.

In the vibrant tapestry of our modern culture, where TV shows and films reign supreme, there exists an assumption that you already possess an intimate understanding of the intricate workings of the illustrious stock market. Discover the untapped potential of the stock market and unlock a world of financial prosperity. Navigating the stock market and its intricate workings can take time and effort for beginners. Gain a profound understanding of the market's inner mechanisms and unravel the enigma behind the rise and fall of stocks. Unlock the secrets of the stock market and arm yourself with essential knowledge before embarking on your investment journey.

Discover the captivating realm of the stock market, where a vast array of stocks eagerly awaits the discerning eye of the public. Immerse yourself in a world of limitless possibilities, where these coveted stocks can be effortlessly bought and sold across many prestigious exchanges.

Discover the art of astute investing - where making a suitable investment is the cornerstone of success. Elevate your financial prowess by embracing the power of a well-diversified portfolio. Unlock the potential to amplify your returns and watch your wealth flourish over time. Discover the art of investing, where the key lies in crafting a financially abundant future.

I once paid about $7500 to attend a weekend business mastermind here in the United States of America. On the first day of the mastermind, as we sat in eager anticipation, waiting for the organizing host and world-renowned business leader to start with some profound business concept, he placed a hammer and some nails in the middle of our round table. He said, "Thank you for taking time out of your busy lives to spend a few days with me, discussing business secrets that will give you an edge over the competition. As we begin, I want to remind you that the best gift you can give your business is to understand, master, and deploy time-tested business principles. In front of you, there's a hammer and some nails. Don't look confused. This is the first big lesson of the day. Before you can ever construct anything of value as an architect, you need the vision in your mind of the type of building you wish to construct, and you need to know the fundamentals of building, complex geometry, design, etc. But you can't construct anything valuable if you don't know how to use basic tools like a hammer and nails, basic laws of setting up a sturdy foundation, etc. Once you know how to work with the basics, you and your team can set up a foundation that holds a bungalow, a mansion, or a skyscraper. The lesson for us as businesspeople is simple. Know the fundamentals first, clarify your vision, and implement those fundamentals. Then you can erect whatever kind of business you desire."

I recall being confused when he started that speech - Staring at the nails and hammer. I thought, "I paid thousands of dollars for a DIY lesson using hammers and nails?" But it made so much sense as I sat there and listened to him. I'm sharing this somewhat unusual and irrelevant story with you because I've seen newbies struggle to create long-term success over the last three decades or more that I've been an active investor. After all, they skipped over the foundations. It's more fun to jump right into the sexy aspects of investing or imagine how rich you will be. Still, I can assure you that learning the fundamentals enables you to grow portfolios that offer financial freedom. So, this book is going to talk about nails and hammers. The basics that you must grasp before any investment work can begin. It will show you the mindset you must have, the strategies you must develop, and the approach you must take with stock investing to save your hard-earned cash. This book is also meant to help you create a good understanding and relationship with money because you will only get very far if you have that. In simple terms, I've written the book I wish I had when I got into this game. You'll hear how I fumbled and failed repeatedly before figuring things out. The painstaking journey I've endured has been worthwhile because it's gotten me to this point and made me all the money I used to dream about, so I am incredibly grateful to be where I am. At the same time, I'm aware I took the slow boat to China. So, this book is a success if I can aid you along your journey, especially now at the beginning, so that you can avoid unnecessary pain and losses.

The big problem in our society is the fact that we want shortcuts. We look at big names like Warren Buffet and want to know the fastest way to get to where he is. And yes, you can learn what he did to help in your execution, but you will lose when you enter the stock market game with that approach. You'll find so-called gurus who dangle that golden carrot in front of you and promise they can get you to that level of success fast and help you avoid the learning curve. I encourage you to run in the opposite direction whenever you encounter such promises. Here's the truth: The learning curve is precisely what you need to become a successful investor. You don't want someone who shows you how to build a skyscraper or, worse still, helps you build a tower when you have no idea what you're doing. Why? Because as soon as you're done, it'll all come crashing down and bury you in it. The learning curve helps you understand what you're doing and why. You need different teachers along your path to help you on your journey of growth and success. Each will help you piece this puzzle together until you reach your ambitions. Given how noisy the world is today, how do you know where to begin or which material to consume and implement first?

Simple. Start by educating yourself and following principle-based guidelines that are time-tested and proven to work. Invest in a teacher, book, course material, or mentorship that you feel in your gut will empower and educate you enough so you can begin this journey with the most confidence and competence. That is my intention for you, and I hope this book helps you meet that end.

The Old World Versus the New World

There was a time when investing was considered a rich man's game. How to get rich isn't a class taught in school, yet it's what we all deserve to learn and experience. A few decades ago, when opportunities like investing were still traditional and inaccessible to people like you and me, amassing wealth was almost a fantasy. My parents and probably your parents were taught that you got a job and worked hard in one position until they retired. Maybe you can retire with enough money to last until you pass. Still, in today's world, thanks to technology and the internet, you and I can easily carve out a path of financial independence regardless of our current vocation, educational background, and even how much savings we have.

Whether you have lots of cash saved up already and a nice six-figure income or not, you can still start today and, in a few years, grow a very healthy portfolio. I know this is possible because that's how I began my journey. I don't come from a highly educated background, and when I made my first investment, I was more novice than many of the people who will read this book. I was smart enough to know I needed to educate myself, but I also knew it would take much effort because my ambitions were huge, and my resources were minimal. I pushed on, learned the craft, took it one step at a time, and more than a decade later, I am an active investor and trader. My investment portfolio in the stock market continues to grow. As you will learn throughout this book, stock investing can give you access to financial opportunities you never even knew possible. You can manifest the lifestyle you've always dreamed of if you choose the path and stick to it until you reap the rewards. Today I am not only buying and holding but also investing in ownership of privately owned businesses that I see real growth opportunities. I also have my toes dipped in some fascinating real estate deals. All these have enabled me to earn even while I sleep and retire from the typical rat race everyone struggles with. I travel overseas for half of the year and work from wherever I want. This used to be a dream that felt more like a fantasy for many years, and because I never gave up on myself, as I hope you won't too, I get to call it my "normal" life.

You Can Live Life and Build Wealth on Your Terms

By committing to the study and implementation of the knowledge contained in this book, you will finally have clarity on what it means to be an investor, what stock market investing is, and how to do it right. You'll have the necessary know-how and tools to help you adequately research and evaluate different stocks to make the right choices. By the end of this book, you'll have everything needed to start and succeed at being a stock investor to forge your path to financial freedom. If you're ready to create real wealth and eliminate confusion about what to do and where to get started, jump into the next chapter, and let's talk investing.

CHAPTER ONE

The Must-Know Language Of Investing

Let's talk about getting rich. When it comes to wealth creation, you have two main options unless you expect to inherit wealth. from a family member. Those two main options are: You either trade your time to make money in some way, shape, or form, or you find a way to have your money (little or large sums) make money for you. The school system only teaches us how to trade time for money. Through our direct involvement, tears, sweat, and blood, we can produce an income that mostly never leads to financial freedom and great wealth. Only a minority have been able to create financial independence following that first option.

The ideal scenario for us is to combine options one and two, especially at the beginning. And, of course, the holy grail we're all searching for is creating enough wealth and financial independence to fully step into option two - having money work for us. That's what billionaires like Mark Cuban and Warren Buffet do, which leaves them time to travel where they want, work when they want, and truly live on their terms. Doesn't that feel great? I know it was one of my biggest desires as a young man growing up. I was sick and tired of seeing how troubled my single mom was.

I vowed to do everything possible to create a better situation for myself. At first, I followed the first option of getting a day job and trading my time for money. I quickly realized that wasn't going to give me the kind of financial freedom I craved, and slowly by slowly, I started to learn about wealth creation. I recall reading my first book on wealth creation, which introduced me to investing. I immediately got hooked, and I've been learning, growing, investing, trading, and creating my wealth ever since. I start this chapter with my story because I need you to realize that investing isn't an instant fix for your financial situation. This is about playing the long game. Investing will allow you to take the driver's seat and become financially independent. But only if you play the game right.

To play the game right, you must understand and align yourself with the game's rules. That's where we're going to start. There needs to be more clarity today, with more and more people talking about investing and trading with little to no proper understanding, and it often leads others astray. So, I know you already want to start learning how to pick and buy stocks, but I need you to exercise a little patience and appreciate the importance of what you're about to do here. And that is, give yourself a crash course on what stock investing means. Even if you think you know, read this entire chapter thoroughly because the first rule of making money as a stock investor is always to be ready and willing to learn. You'll lose if you're a "know it " in stock investing. You will win if you're a "learn it all" in stock investing. It is that simple.

What is Investing, and How Many Classes Are There?

Investing is very dynamic and evolving, so it's prudent that a newbie grasps the complete picture of investing before jumping into one. Although this book is focused on stock investing, there are various other ways you can invest, depending on your personality, goals, and risk tolerance.

To state it, investing is putting money to work for you. It is using your hard-earned money to purchase an asset, interest, or any mechanism that you believe will generate income and profit in the future. There are three types of investments that anyone can participate in, namely, Ownership, Lending, and Cash equivalents.

Ownership Investment

It's the one most people imply when they call themselves an investor. Ownership investments are the most volatile and profitable investment class; our book will focus on it—specifically, stock investment. Aside from owning stocks, you can also invest in starting and running a business. You can invest in precious objects such as gold or collectibles such as a signed LeBron James Jersey. If you buy these particular objects and collectibles intending to resell them for a profit, that is considered an ownership investment. The last example of an ownership type of investment is real estate, meaning apartments, houses, or other dwellings you buy to rent out or resell. Here comes an important distinction. Mortgaging a place to live in is not considered an ownership investment. It shouldn't be purchased with the expectation of profit, even if it will be appreciated with time. So, if you think your mortgage is an asset or investment, think again.

Lending Investment

It's a lower risk than ownership investments, that's for sure. However, the returns are usually less. As a leading investor, you essentially take on the bank's role. Examples of lending investments include bonds, which we'll discuss shortly, and savings accounts. Even if you only have a regular savings account, you're still considered an investor because you're essentially lending money to the bank. Of course, the return is relatively low, and you're probably not getting wealthy from this investment. Still, the risk factor is also close to zero because of the Federal Deposit Insurance Corporation (FDIC) that covers your back.

Cash Equivalents

These are highly liquid investments, meaning they easily convert back into cash. These types of investments are as good as having cash in your pocket. Examples include money market funds, which, although they have low returns (usually between 1% -2%), also have low risk, and writing a check out of money market accounts is as simple as using your checking account.

As mentioned, you're here to learn the basics of stock market investing, which falls under ownership investment. But before we dive into everything you need to know about stocks, let's touch briefly on some of the previously mentioned examples, such as bonds, cash investments, and real estate, as well as other alternatives such as mutual funds, exchange-traded funds (EFTs), hedge funds, etc.

Bonds Investment

The simplest way to understand bond investing is to consider it a kind of I.O.U between lender and borrower. In this case, you, as an investor, will buy a bond, which is a fixed-income instrument that represents the load given to either a corporation or government agency, and they are obliged to pay you a fixed interest rate in exchange for using your capital. Bond prices are inversely correlated with interest rates, meaning when integrated rates rise, bond prices fall, and bond prices rise when they drop.

The borrower, also known as the bond issuer, usually provides a bond that includes the loan terms, interest payments that will be made, and the time at which the loaned funds, aka bond principal, must be paid back. This "time" is known as the maturity date.

All bonds have a maturity date determining when the principal amount must be paid back in full or risk default. Think of bond investing as a way for you to lend money to big organizations and the government. They usually use this instrument to borrow money to fund projects, build schools, etc. Bonds are among the top three common investment types. The other two are stocks and cash.

One of the great things about bond investing is that you can hold a bond only some of the way through to its maturity because, in most cases, you can sell it to other investors.

Cash Investment

If you are only interested in a temporary fix for your cash, meaning you need somewhere safe to keep your money for whatever reason, then this type of investment might be right for you. Cash investments are very low-level risk investments usually insured by Federal Deposit Insurance Corporation (FDIC). As an investor, you get a short-term (90 days or less) investment that is simple, easy to execute, and can provide a return in interest payments. Unfortunately, this return type is low compared to other investment types. I consider this one of the safest ways to preserve your capital. Certificates of deposit (CDs) and Money market accounts (MMA) are examples of cash investments.

Stock Investment

This book discusses what stock is and how the stock market works. But to give you a lay of the land, understand that stock investment is when you purchase shares of stocks (equity) in a company to benefit from a company's success. Think of it as owning a small piece of that company. Usually, the benefits come from an increase in the stock's price and through dividends. Only and always buy a stock that you feel fully convinced must increase in value with time. When you buy stocks, you are considered a stock investor and can be called a shareholder. If you do a good job choosing a stock that increases in value over time, you can sell the store for a profit.

Public companies sell their stock through the stock market exchange, e.g., New York Stock Exchange or Nasdaq. Investors buy and sell these shares among themselves through stockbrokers. Depending on the kind of stock you own, you may or may not have voting rights at a shareholders' meeting.

If you want to succeed as an investor, I encourage you to buy and hold for a long time. As the book unfolds, we'll learn how to make money in stock investing.

Mutual Funds

A mutual fund is a common type of investing that I encourage every young, ambitious person to consider doing. It's a relatively low-capital investment and can be a great segue to stocks and other high-risk investments. Investor.gov defines a mutual fund as a company that pools money from many investors and invests the money in securities such as stocks, bonds, and short-term debt. The combined holdings of the mutual fund are known as its portfolio. So, consider it as joining fellow investors to pool your money to purchase securities. When you invest, you get to own shares representing your part ownership in the fund, which determines your income. The good news is that you don't need much money to get started, and you still get to diversify because mutual funds allow you to purchase different kinds of securities with your capital. You also don't need to manage the investment yourself because there are professionals who care, allocate, and distribute the pooled investment into bonds, stocks, and other securities. With mutual funds, you can earn money through dividend payments, increased NAV, and capital gains distribution. One of the things I like about mutual fund shares is that they are redeemable. So, as an investor, you can always sell your shares back to the fund whenever you wish. They are also highly liquid so that you can convert a mutual fund into cash within a few days.

Exchange-Traded Funds

An exchange-traded fund, often called an EFT, is a collection of securities, such as stocks, that trade daily on the exchange market just as stores do. They are like a mutual fund, except they trade throughout the day and mirror stocks' buy-sell behavior, making them volatile. The value of an EFT can drastically change during a trading day. One of the things that makes an EFT special is that it can hold multiple underlying assets, which means you can quickly diversify because you can own hundreds or even thousands of stocks across various industries if you choose. Some investors prefer to focus on a particular industry or sector, while others prefer funds that offer different U.S. assets. Others still like to get funds that have a global outlook. Depending on whether you want to use your EFT to generate income, hedge, or partly offset risk in one of your portfolios, or for various other reasons, there's a suitable EFT that you can invest in. I find EFTs among the most popular type of investment because of the flexibility and ease of trading, not to mention the broad coverage they offer. An example of a famous EFT is the SPDR S&P 500 EFT (SPY), which tracks the S&P 500 Index.

Hedge Funds and Private Equity Funds

Hedge funds are special and considered by the market as alternative investments because they use different investment strategies to generate "alpha" (returns). They are usually set up as private investment limited partnerships open to a limited number of accredited investors. I don't encourage this for a beginner working with a small budget, as hedge funds require a significant initial minimum investment. The other thing is that your funds won't be liquid because, in most cases, you'd have to go through the lock-up period (meaning your money is inaccessible) often a year or more. Your withdrawal ability is also limited to certain specified intervals, such as quarterly or bi-annually.

On the other hand, private equity deals with funds and investors that directly invest in private companies or engage in buyouts of public companies, resulting in the delisting of public equity. A private equity fund consists of Limited Partners who typically own 99% of shares in a fund with limited liability and General Partners who own 1% of shares with total liability. Venture capitalists are a great example of this type of investment because they finance companies and start-ups through this form of private equity.

These are only a few conventional and alternative investments you can engage in to grow your wealth. As you've seen, some are easy to start, requiring little capital and offering low-risk, low returns. Others need lots of investment capital and high-risk tolerance. Regardless of your ambitions, I suggest you start slow and straightforward, even if you have more than enough capital to engage in activities such as venture capitalism. The reason is that learning the language, the rules of investing, and getting your hands dirty in a small way gives you priceless experience and insight that you can apply even as a VC. That's why I now encourage you to switch all your attention to stock investing. It's the best starting point any severe investor can have. So, let's start at the beginning.

What is a Stock?

Stocks, sometimes known as equities, provide shareholders with a stake in a publicly traded corporation. It's an interest in the company, and if you hold most of the shares, you have complete control over how the company functions. The stock market is a collection of stocks the public can buy and sell on various exchanges.

Where does stock originate? Public Companies issue stock to fund their operations. Investors that believe the company will succeed in the future purchase those stock issues. Dividends and share price appreciation are distributed to shareholders. They may also see their investment dwindle or vanish if the company runs out of funds.

A stock is a certificate issued by the appropriate governing body that states you own a piece of a company. When a company needs money, it has two main options for acquiring cash. It can borrow or raise money by selling some of its shares to interested investors. These shares are what we call "stocks" or equities.

When you buy a stock, you become the owner of shares in that company. It's an investment (a stock investment) that enables you to claim ownership. Stock is the name given to the valuable certificates issued by share capital companies to their shareholders to document their shares and partnerships. Stocks also represent a property or partnership. They are bought and sold on the stock exchange, although some can be privately acquired.

What Is the Stock Market?

The stock market is an aftermarket in which shareholders can sell their shares to investors looking to buy them. This is done on a stock exchange like the New York Stock Exchange or the Nasdaq. Traders used to go to a physical site — the exchange's floor — to deal in the past, but now almost all trading is done online.

When newscasters say, "The market was up today," they usually mean the performance of the S&P 500 or the Dow Jones Industrial Average. The S&P 500 index comprises 500 big publicly traded Companies in the United States, whereas the Dow includes the 30 largest corporations. These track the performance of stock collections and illustrate how they performed on that day of trading as well as over time.

However, while the Dow and the S&P 500 are referred to as "the market," they are stock indexes. These indexes represent some of the largest corporations in the United States, but they do not represent the entire market, which consists of thousands of publicly traded companies.

Investopedia defines the stock market as the collection of markets and exchanges where regular buying, selling, and issuing publicly held company shares occur. These financial activities are administered through institutionalized formal exchanges or over-the-counter (OTC) marketplaces operating under regulations. A more straightforward way to understand the stock market can be found if you consider that it's often used to refer to one of the major stock market indexes, such as the S&P 500 (an overall index because it represents so many blue-chip companies) or the Dow Jones Industrial Average (one of the oldest stock market index and also one of the smallest with only 30 companies). There's also the Nasdaq Composite index, which represents thousands of companies on the Nasdaq stock market. The Nasdaq composite is one of the most diverse indexes because it has more companies than the S&P 500 or Dow Jones. There's also Russel 2000, Financial Times Stock Exchange 100, etc.

You might read or see a headline on the news that says the stock market has closed for the day or has moved lower. Usually, this means that stock market indexes have moved up or that they've lost value. Because it's not easy to track every stock, these indexes include a section of the stock market, and their performance is viewed as a representative of the whole market. The up-and-down movement you'll hear about informs you whether the stocks increase or decrease in value in the marketplace. Of course, as investors, we buy and sell supplies expecting to profit through this up-and-down movement in stock prices.

How the stock market works

The stock market works similarly to an auction house in that buyers and sellers negotiate prices and make trades. It's really that simple. Where does this negotiation and business take place? We call it the marketplace. It's a network of exchanges regulated by government-approved organizations, and the most important ones here in the U.S. are the New York Stock Exchange and Nasdaq.

Approximately sixty stock exchanges are worldwide, but you'll probably only ever hear about the following five major ones. New York Stock Exchange (NYSE), London Stock Exchange (LSE), Tokyo Stock Exchange (TSE), Shanghai Stock Exchange (SSE), and Hong Kong Stock Exchange (HKEX).

Companies looking to raise funds will list shares of their stock on an exchange (a process called IPO which stands for initial public offering), and then investors like you and me get to buy those shares. Once we obtain the claims, we can sell these stocks amongst ourselves, playing the game of buying and selling, leading to a supply-demand scenario. The exchange tracks the supply and demand of each listed stock, which helps determine the price for each security. This is done through algorithms that take care of the price calculations or the levels at which stock market participants, i.e., traders and investors, can buy or sell.

As the buyer, you will offer what's known as a "bid," i.e., the highest amount you're willing to pay, which is usually lower than what the seller wants in exchange, aka the "ask." The difference created between your bid and the seller's ask is called the bid-ask spread. That's a critical term to remember, as you'll often hear it. For a trade to occur, you, as the buyer, must increase your price, or the seller must decrease the ask. Thus, the game starts between the Bulls and the Bears.

It would be best to remember that trading took place in a physical marketplace for a long time. That came with its own set of limitations and advantages. Nowadays, however, trading has gone electronic, and thanks to the advent of the Internet and online stockbrokers, stock trading has evolved and become more accessible. Each trade happens on a stock-by-stock basis, but overall, stock prices usually fluctuate because of news, political events, economic reports, and other factors.

Chapter Two

Understanding the Type of Stocks and Stock Tables

Now that you know what a stock is and understand the stock market, let's thoroughly understand the different types of stores you can invest in. There are two types of supplies: common stock and preferred stock.

Common Stock

Common stock represents your funds and shares of ownership in the corporation you've invested in. As a joint stock owner, you are entitled to both the risk and rewards of ownership, but your liability is limited to the capital you contribute. With common stock, you have income rights meaning a residual claim on the company's earnings. You also have the right to elect the company's board of directors at a general meeting and vote on various corporate policies. In the event of liquidation of the company, you would be entitled to receive the remaining funds and assets of the company assuming all creditors, denture holders, and preferred stockholders have been paid. What you receive will be proportional to the number of shares you own. One last thing you should know about being a joint stock investor is that you will have pre-emptive rights. That implies you can purchase the company's stock before it becomes publicly available. I like to think of it as getting first dibs.

Preferred Stock

It is like the common stock with this crucial differentiator in many ways. And that is that with preferred stock, you would have no voting rights; however, you do get to claim more on the company's assets and income. So, when it comes to having a voice in the company or helping to shape its future, you have no say as a preferred stock investor. Some like to equate this investing to bond investing because, as an investor, you are usually guaranteed a fixed dividend in perpetuity. In some instances, you can even get repayment of capital in the event of bankruptcy or liquidation. But unlike bonds, this may or may not have a maturity period. The dividend yield of preferred stock is calculated as the dividend dollar amount divided by the stock price. It is often based on the par value before a preferred stock is offered. Usually, it will be calculated as a percentage of the current market price after it begins trading. If you're a preferred stock investor, you claim a company's assets and earnings more during liquidation. Also, regarding dividends, the preferred stock gets priority over common stock, and their tips are usually higher than those issued for common stock.

Another essential thing to know about preferred stock is that the issuer can redeem the shares from you after a predetermined price at a significant premium over the purchase price. You also can convert to a fixed number of common shares, something an everyday stock investor needs to be more capable of doing. So, while they are similar, subtle differences make them unique and valuable. Depending on your objectives, weigh the pros and cons before deciding which type of stock to invest in. Aside from knowing these two types of stock, you also need to understand what stores do.

What do stocks do?

As an investor, stocks are intended to make you a profit. Of course, you need to make the right choice and invest wisely. They are proof that you are in partnership with a company. The most critical rights stocks give you is the right to get a share of the profit. You get the best out of a company or business without participating in the bureaucracy, management, and administration involved in running a profitable business.

Understanding Stock Tickers and Stock Tables

To understand stock tickers, you must first know what a ticker is. I'm sure you've seen that scrolling text at the bottom of a business news show or those big electronic LED screens that display the rolling market in real-time, often used by traders to keep track of stock in movie scenes. And today, if you visit any financial website, it's likely that you will find the exact scrolling text with overwhelming information at the top of the site. Most people tune out these streaming data because they often appear confusing and never-ending. However, this data is crucial to us as investors, so you'll want to train your brain to process and understand that information. In essence, that piece of information is what's known as a ticker. A tick is created whenever there's a change in the price of the security in the marketplace, whether that movement is up or down. The stock ticker (which has its roots in the world of telegraphy and was patented and modified by Thomas Edison himself) automatically displays the ticks during the trading session. Given the enormous volume of foreign securities, what you'll often see, especially on television, are a few of the most prestigious companies and indexes. Before you get overwhelmed, here's a simple way of understanding and reading stock tickers.

For publicly traded companies, the ticker symbol with an abbreviation of the company's name will appear on the stock ticker instead of the company's full name. You'll notice that most ticker symbols are very close to the company name. For example, McDonald's ticker symbol is MCD.

Some companies, however, like to get creative with their symbols since they can pick whatever symbol they desire. That's why the Cheesecake Factory's ticker symbol is CAKE, and Sealy Corporation (a mattress company) uses the symbol ZZ.

Another thing to note regarding ticker symbols is that different stock markets will have their own rules on how many letters the logo can have. For example, companies on the New York Stock Exchange have up to three characters, while on Nasdaq are allowed to have four or five characters. At some point, these different ticker symbol rules for each stock market posed a challenge that frustrated many investors. When a company moves from one stock market to another, e.g., from NYSE to Nasdaq, which is very common, it would be forced to change the ticker symbol to conform to the new rules. This created much confusion for investors, and so in 2007, the SEC (securities exchange commission) decided that companies could keep their ticker symbol if it had three characters. Any company with a one or two-character ticker symbol can keep the same sign even after moving to a different exchange.

Below is a mini list of leading companies you'll mostly see on the ticker symbol on any given day with their accompanying ticker symbol.

Apple - (AAPL)

Amazon - (AMZN)

Anthem - (ANTM)

American Airlines Group, Inc. - (AAL)

Google - (GOOG)

IBM - (IBM)

Walmart - (WMT)

JP Morgan Chase - (JPM)

Johnson & Johnson - (JNJ)

Intel Corp. - (INTC)

Visa - (V)

McDonald - (MCD)

Tesla, Inc. - (TSLA)

Facebook, Inc. - (FB)

What does the stock ticker data tell you?

Let's take an example of GOOG 12.4M 16655 ^ 12.50

GOOG - shows you the ticker symbol. These characters help us identify a company on the stock exchange. A three-letter sign means the stock trades on the NYSE. Four letters may indicate it traded on NASDAQ. In this case, our ticker tells us this is Google's parent company.

12.4M - shows you the volume of shares traded. It's how many stock shares are being sold that day. The volume amount is abbreviated as "K" (indicating a thousand), "M" (indicating a million), and "B" (indicating billion). This can change and fluctuate throughout the trading day.

1665 - this shows you the trade value. It refers to the price per share or the last bid price. Like the share volume, this can change rapidly and fluctuate throughout the trading day.

(^) - This shows the change in direction, indicating whether the stock is trading higher or lower than when the market closed the previous day.

12.50 - this shows you the change amount. It details how much the stock price has changed since the market closed the day before and includes both dollars and cents.

You might also see a percentage of the price change in some instances. Aside from the letters and numbers on the screen, you must pay attention to the color. Green indicates the stock is trading higher than when it closed the previous day. Red means it's trading lower than when the market closed the day before. White or blue indicates there was no change from the last day.

Stock Tables

Before considering yourself a real investor (yes, even before you can expect to make money), you need to know how to read stock tables. It's one of the first lessons you must immerse yourself in and practice over time until you become masterful. Stock tables give you insight into a particular stock's performance. When you know what you're doing, reading a stock table can help you spot opportunities and avoid losses. They can help you determine whether to invest in that stock or not. Depending on where you get your stock tables from, they might vary in the information and layout; however, there are certain critical pieces of information all stock tables must contain. Let's go over these.

Name and Ticker Symbol: This column tells you the company name. It's often written in total, and the stock ticker symbol will be present, which, as we said before, are often abbreviations of the company name or something that represents the company somehow.

52-Week High: This column tells you the highest price that stock has reached in the most recent fifty-two-week period.

52-Week Low: This column tells you the lowest price that stock has reached in the most recent fifty-two-week period.

52-Week Range: Within one column, it details the lowest and highest price the stock reached over the past fifty-two weeks.

Volume: This column indicates the number of shares traded that day. For example, if you see 1000, it means only 1000 shares were sold that day.

Average Volume: This amount will tell you about the average volume over a specified period (e.g., three months or a year) and is used to give you a more in-depth look into how the stock is trading.

Previous Close: This column shows the amount of the stock price traded at the last day's close.

Open: The stock price will be shown at the market's opening.

Day's Range: It will indicate price fluctuations of the stock on that day.

P/E: This column represents the ratio between the stock price and the company's earnings. P/E stands for price per earnings and usually gives us a strong indication of whether a stock holds good value. Pay close attention to this metric.

Day Last: This column shows you how trading ended for a particular stock on the day represented by the table.

Net Change: This column will help you understand how the stock price ended on that day compared with the trading price at the end of the previous trading day.

Dividend: This column shows you the amount you will receive in a tip per year, per share of stock. For example, if you see 1.00, you'll earn $1 per share of stock annually as an investor. The dividend may be paid out monthly, quarterly, yearly, etc.

Yield: This column shows the percentage of that dividend on the stock price. The result is important for income investors, and we calculate it by dividing the annual premium by the current stock price.

In some cases, you might find dividends and yield in the same column; in others, it may not appear. Whenever you don't see a dividend column, it indicates that the company doesn't offer dividends.

The High, Low, Open, And Close of Stock Charts

Stock charts are price charts that show you a particular stock's price plotted over a given timeframe. You can get your hands on daily, weekly, monthly, quarterly, and annual stock charts.

Day traders can access even more miniaturized charts, known as intraday charts, which can be as short as 5 minutes. But as an investor, you don't need to concern yourself too much with intraday or even daily charts because your focus is to spot long-term trends. Therefore, weekly and monthly stock charts are the best charts to start reading. Aside from learning to interpret the volume, stock symbol, and the specific exchange it trades on, you also want to get good at understanding the price movement. That's where price change comes into play. Regardless of the different flavors and styles of stock charts, each one will always display the price. The better you interpret this, the easier it will be to see the trendlines and make profitable investing decisions.

The price change includes four key data points: The high, low, open, and close, all from that day's trading activities. The "high" indicates the highest price, and the "low" means the lowest price during that session. "Open" indicates the price at the start of the day, and naturally, "close" shows you the price at the end of that trading day.

Stock Market Investing Terminology for Beginners

You must know the most used stock market terminology to become a great trader. Below are the main ones you want to start practicing and quizzing yourself on so they can become part of your daily vocabulary.

Arbitrage - The buying and selling of the same security in different markets and price points.

Annual Report - A report prepared by a company (intended to impress shareholders) that contains information about the company, including cash flow, management strategy, and financial situation.

Ask - The lowest price a seller will accept when selling a stock.

Bid - The money a trader will pay per share for a given stock.

Bear - An investor who believes a particular stock or the market will decline.

Bull - An investor who believes a particular stock or the market will rise. This is, of course, the opposite of a bear.

Bull Market - Trading jargon used when the stock market is in a prolonged period of increasing stock prices.

Bear Market - Trading jargon for the stock market being in a downward trend. Aka, the opposite of a bull market. When a stock price plummets, we say it's very bearish.

Beta - This is a measurement of the relationship between the price of a stock and the movement of the whole market.

Bid-Ask Spread - The difference between the bid and the ask of a given trade. It's that gap between what the buyer wants to spend and what the seller is willing to accept for a business.

Blue Chip - A company with a history of stable earnings, regular and increasing dividends, and an impeccable balance sheet.

Capital Gain - The profit obtained from selling any capital asset where the selling price exceeds the investment's purchase price.

Close - This is when the stock exchange closes to trading. For example, the NYSE and Nasdaq close at 4 pm Eastern, with after-hours trading continuing until 8 pm.

Dividend - A portion of a company's earnings paid to shareholders or individuals that own that company's stock. It is typically paid on a quarterly or annual basis.

An Exchange is where different investments are traded—for example, the New York Stock Exchange.

Index - A benchmark used as a reference marker for traders and portfolio managers. Examples include Standard & Poor's 500 and Dow Jones Industrial Average.

IPO - This is for Initial Public Offering, the first sale or offering of a stock by a company to the public.

Liquidity refers to how easily you can get into and out of a stock.

Market Capitalization - Commonly referred to as a market cap, it is what the market thinks a company's value is. You determine market cap by multiplying the current price per share with the number of shares outstanding.

Portfolio - A group of financial assets such as stocks, bonds, cash equivalents, commodities, currencies, and their fund counterparts (mutual funds, ETFs, etc.)

Quote - This is the latest trading price on a stock.

Stock Symbol - This symbol represents a publicly traded company on a stock exchange. It can be between one and four alphabetical characters: for example, Walmart.

Is WMT.

Volatility - This implies the price movement of a particular stock or the stock market. Highly volatile stocks have extreme daily up-and-down activities and wide intraday trading ranges.

Volume - This is the number of shares of stock traded during a particular time, typically measured in average daily trading volume.

Yield - Refers to the measure of the return on an investment received from a dividend payment. To calculate profit, divide the annual dividend amount by the price paid for the stock.

CHAPTER THREE

Why Should You Invest in Stocks?

We all enter the game of stock market investing for various reasons. Some of us are young and just starting in life, and we're intelligent (and ambitious) enough to realize financial freedom won't come from getting a salary with benefits. Others take a while to figure this out and get to the family planning (middle-aged) phase of their life, only to realize they need to do something if they want better retirement conditions. And, of course, some are already approaching retirement, and it's dawning on them that a new source of steady and increasing income is the only way they can enjoy the years to come. Investing in stocks is a great decision regardless of age, current income, or ambitions. And it all begins with a solid plan and your first dollar. The only way to grow wealth in modern times and achieve financial freedom is to either work hard and hope it will happen or take personal responsibility, learn to invest, and make your luck. As we said before, you can invest in many ways, but I strongly recommend investing in the stock market because of how well it has worked for others and me. The risks are higher than other investment forms, but the rewards and the return on your investment make it worthwhile. If you know what you're doing, stock market investing will help you achieve your financial goals.

One of the main things I enjoy about stock market investing compared to other types of investing, such as real estate, is how easy it is to buy shares of companies. All you need is a broker, a financial planner, or online, and they'll hook you up with an account, after which you're good to go. I also like the fact that you can sell your stock at any time. In trading jargon, we call it "liquidity." So, for example, if you need money fast, you can turn your shares into cash and, in most cases, with meager transaction costs. As the economy grows, your wealth will increase if you're an intelligent investor. And since investors buy low and sell high over prolonged periods, your ability to spot and invest in fast-growing companies that appreciate over time means you can amass wealth relatively fast. This is especially true if you invest in a company growing steadily and paying out healthy dividends. Of course, that's not to say there are no risks. Any investment carries certain risks, and it's up to you to determine how healthy your appetite is for risk-taking. With stock market investing, you could lose your entire investment. If that scares you and makes you sick, I recommend forgoing stock investing altogether and opting for something like bond investing. You also need to know that stock investing is a long-term game.

You can't expect quick wins and must keep your emotions in check. Your ability to discipline yourself and keep your emotions out of decision-making is vital because stock prices rise and fall by the second on any trading day. Volatility and price fluctuations are states you must get used to. I usually encourage my clients to avoid continually looking at the price dips of stocks. In your plan, ensure you include a regular schedule for updating yourself on price fluctuations, but it is to a minimum.

Creating Income and Profit

For many who don't understand the game, making money as a stock investor is about picking the right stock, trading rapidly, and continuously obsessing about the indexes while glued to a screen. That's an excellent way to miss out on earning a lot of money. Why do I say this?

The industry benchmark for the stock market's average returns is 10%, which is impressive compared to other alternatives. However, that only applies to confident investors. Most people never make that much, and it isn't because the market is unfair. The reason is that most investors behave like day traders. They need to be more short-term oriented and stay invested long enough for their effort to pay off. So, what is the secret to creating income and profit? Benjamin Graham said it best. "The real money in investing will have to be made - as most of it has been in the past - not out of buying and selling but our owning and holding securities, receiving interest and dividends and benefiting from their long-term increase in value." In other words, your time in the market will determine your overall performance. If you keep moving in and out of the stock market, the chances of doing it at the worst possible time and messing with your annual return are high. The more time, the more opportunity you have for your investments to increase because many companies tend to increase their profits over time. That, in turn, leads to higher stock prices, which translates into higher returns for investors owning the stock. So again, increased income and profitability as a stock investor is very much a game of dividends and yield. If you're the kind of trader that likes to trade in and out of the market daily, weekly, or monthly, then kiss those dividends goodbye because you probably won't own the stock at critical points that would enable you to capture pay-outs. That's why it's essential to figure out what kind of investor you'll be, what you care about, and what financial goals matter to you.

Financial Goals

While it's essential to become a successful stock investor, I've found nothing makes that journey of amateur to mastery more bearable than knowing why you're doing it. Chasing after money for the sake of it never brought anyone fulfillment and happiness, and it never will. So, before you commit fully to this journey, do a self-check, and figure out your financial goals and why you need to attain them. What's driving you? What's your why? How much money do you equate with financial freedom? We are all different, and what might be little money for me could be some- one's financial dreams come true. Take the time to identify your financial goals and write those down clearly. Here's a remarkable statement to help you align with your goals.

I want to succeed in my stock investment activities and grow a healthy portfolio to accomplish my goals and become financially independent. My main income/profit goal in the next five years of my investment activities is to have an exact number and state why I want this amount.

Identifying your short-term, intermediate, and long-term goals is also essential. Long-term goals would be classified as anything that needs funding five or more years from now. Intermediate goals will be the financial goals that need funding for two to four years, and short-term goals are less than two years from now. I'll remind you again that stock investment is best suited for people with significant long-term goals, such as financial independence or paying for a long-term project, etc.

Make It Your Business

If there's one mistake I want you to avoid that so many of us have been guilty of (me included), it is the inability to treat investing as a serious business. Stock investment is a serious business; those who take this approach will always win. Suppose you want to avoid suffering unnecessary loss or missing out on getting paid high dividends. In that case, you'll have to avoid taking advice from friends, forums, articles, and gossip magazines and instead educate yourself about stock market investing and how to do it right. One of the shifts I made when I realized I wasn't an investor is I stopped actively trading. For a while, I bought and sold nothing. I cut out the time I spent in forums and chat rooms and instead took up courses and read books about various companies and why they were successful. Companies that I wanted to invest in, like Wal-Mart. For about six months, I was busy learning how to manage a business at my local college, and over that training, I saw investing in a whole new light. I started to understand the fundamentals of running any business, and today, I've implemented many of those lessons across the different companies I now run over a decade later. Some of the things you want to start understanding about taking this new "business" approach include:

You are creating a business plan for yourself with appropriate goals and objectives. Clearly outline the program you will execute. Make sure it's thorough and details what you will invest in. Will it be stocks only or stocks and bonds? Will you only buy stores that pay dividends or mix and match?

Identify the income and profit streams, how you intend to pay yourself and your broker, and any mentor or teacher you need. In other words, determine your expenses and ensure they align with your income projections.

You also need to develop the ability to shift from strategic thinking to tactical implementation. Strategic thinking is the ability to understand the different possible market "conditions" and how various tools can be better suited for specific seasons in the market. It's also essential to develop a sound tracking system to track all transactions and their profit and loss, identify trends, see what works and what doesn't, etc.

Stocks Versus Inflation

Inflation tracks the price of goods and services and shrinks the dollar's purchasing power. That means when inflation rises, you can purchase fewer goods with the same amount of money, and as input prices go up, revenue and profits go down. The result is economic stagnation as things slow down until stability returns. Inflation is bad for everyone, including investors, because we pay more for less. The good news is that when it comes to stock market investing, you can protect yourself and your investments because, in theory, a company's revenue and earnings should grow at the same rate as inflation. If you're holding cash equivalents or similar investments, you are more likely to experience the hard blows of inflation. Still, if you've invested in the right stocks, you should be able to hedge off inflation seasons.

CHAPTER FOUR

The Basics You Need to Know About the Stock Market

When it comes to the stock market, there are two fundamental terms you need to understand and differentiate. They are trading and investing. These two terms are not synonymous, and it will be wise to understand what each word means and which of the two you want to focus on. This book is written specifically for investors of stock, not traders. There's a huge difference. Some people are successful in trading; others are better at investing; even fewer people are successful and naturally gifted to be great at both. You must deploy enough self-awareness to know which is best for you. I assume you know that being a stock investor is the right choice. So, let me give you a brief overview of some vital stock market concepts, including the difference between trading and investing in stocks.

Important stock market concepts that every newbie should know. Trading versus investing in a stock. The most significant difference between these two activities is the duration of a position. As a trader, you're only focused on participating in the game for the shortest time possible. You're looking for quick returns, so things like dividends and yields may need to be more relevant. As an investor, you care a lot about dividends and work. Your investments are generally meant to last several years. Although both a trader and investor are putting their money in the game expecting to gain profit, a trader's expectation may be as short as a few seconds up to a few weeks.

Conversely, an investor is most likely expecting their return within a year, a few years, or even a few decades. But that doesn't mean you can't buy and sell an investment for a profit next week. Just know that if you do, that's considered a trade.

Only when you purchase a security to keep it for a long time to experience the company's growth would you be considered an investor. So again, there is much overlap between these two terms, but it comes down to intention and timetable. The other thing I need to break down for you is the difference between stock trading and investing to avoid confusion once you enter the game.

The main differences between these two concepts are the return on investment, the capital investment, the risks involved, and the psychology needed to excel in either one of these activities. With stock market trading, you buy and sell shares in a company or derivatives based on shares in a company, expecting a profit. It is one of the most popular investments, and you would earn money in one of these two ways:

Price movement - when there's more demand than supply in the shares of a company, the prices usually rise. Investors in shares try to take advantage of these situations.

Dividends - as an investor, you are, in fact, a partial owner of the company, so you get your cut of the company's earnings and profits depending on the type of shares you own and the terms and conditions around it.

The two main ways to trade are becoming a day trader or a swing trader. Both have advantages and disadvantages. They also have equally long learning curves, so don't fool yourself into thinking you can learn both simultaneously. As a stock market trader, you must develop "good timing" skills and quickly act whenever the right opportunity comes. This skill benefits you from short-term market price changes, enabling quick profits.

Stock market investing

As we said, this is about investing in creating wealth long-term. So, what you will need is the skill of increasing prosperity and wealth through growing the interest and dividends of the company whose stocks you keep. I define the long-term as anything beyond three years. As an investor, you don't have to worry so much about daily price fluctuations of the stock price or the volatility of the market- place on a day-to-day basis. This means you can control risk a bit more than a trader.

Capital Gains

Capital gains are the profit you earn as an investor when you sell an asset like stocks, bonds, etc. When an asset's selling price (investment or property) exceeds the buying price, the result is capital gain. Another way to look at this is by viewing it as the difference between cost price (also known as the base cost of the investment) and selling price. You get capital gain when the cost and selling prices are high. By contrast, when the cost price is high and the selling price is low, we call that capital loss.

A capital gain can be short-term (a year or less) or long-term (more than a year) and must be declared in the income tax. Short-term investments in collectibles are taxed as short-term capital gains at ordinary income tax rates, while long-term investments in collectibles are taxed at 28% fixed. If your investment results in capital loss, that loss may lower your taxes a bit, but in general, capital loss isn't eligible for tax benefits. Capital gains have tax consequences on your investment, meaning your tax will depend on your tax bracket, asset class, and how long you have the asset. To understand the topic of tax better, I recommend you invest time and resources in a good accountant so they can help you figure out how to play the always confusing game of taxes as an investor. As of the writing of this book, governments around the world are trying to define Crypto for tax purposes better and whether they are like stocks, commodities, or currencies.

Dividend

A dividend is the annual profit distribution from stock corporations to their shareholders. This means that the companies distribute part of their profits to the shareholders every year. This "profit distribution" typically happens once a year. Every year all publicly traded companies get to decide whether they will pay out dividends and how high they will be. If a bonus pay-out was made in the previous year, it could go up or down, and sometimes it could fall back to zero, in which case no dividends would be given to shareholders. The more successful a company is, the higher the chances of getting reliable yearly bonuses. The stock-issuing corporation usually decides the amount of the dividend to be paid out on the day of the general meeting. Then it is paid to the shareholders a day later. As an investor, this is the treat you should be looking forward to, and it's your job to do your research well enough so you can own shares of a company that offers reliable dividends each year. Not all companies pay dividends, so if you find bonus payments attractive, pick a stock with this additional offer.

In recent years where low growth and low-interest rates seem to be the typical environment, getting stock that pays dividends has become a more attractive solution because they form a vital part of the return we get on a stock market investment in the long run. Why? Because, with dividends, we can invest more by buying more shares, especially if we reinvest your profits properly. As a rule of thumb, I teach all my students and clients to reinvest their dividends until their portfolio grows to a desirable size. And if you feel like you can't reinvest all your profits because you have other obligations, that's okay, too; take a small portion and reinvest that because something is better than nothing. With dividends, you can also absorb possible risks or even losses at low moments when the market is weak. Another great reason to invest in dividend stocks is that most dividend payments have distinct tax advantages. Speak to your accountant to understand precisely how you can benefit.

Risks in Stock Market Investing and How to Minimize the Risk

All investment types carry a certain level of risk, but I'm sure you've heard the horror stories of people who lost everything when their stock investments went sour. Occasional market recessions and the natural volatility of stocks do not help instill confidence back into aspiring investors. So, I know there's a lot to worry about, especially as a first-time investor, but I can assure you that everything worthwhile in life will always carry a fair share of risk. If you have no appetite for risk and your personality and emotions are not resilient enough to withstand threats, consider becoming an investor. Whenever you stand to make a profit, there's always a chance that things might go in the opposite direction. If you know you want to do this but want to mitigate or minimize loss as much as possible, the following paragraphs should help you increase your confidence.

Reducing risk when it comes to stock investing is about getting educated about the stock, understanding the market, and thoroughly knowing what you're getting into before entering any position. Then, it's a matter of common sense, the right plan, and patience. Before determining what stocks to invest in, I recommend evaluating your potential investment and analyzing these high-risk areas:

Inflation risk

Inflation risk, aka purchasing power risk, rises when the cash you have today gets you less than it did yesterday. A recession usually leads to high inflation, which negatively impacts investments.

How to minimize risk:

Stock investing helps you mitigate risk as an investor because companies tend to adjust prices to the inflation rate. Something else you can consider doing is investing in U.S. Treasury inflation-protected securities, as this will mitigate inflation risk.

Liquidity risk

Liquidity risk arises when you buy an investment, decide to sell it to prevent or minimize loss, but quickly realize no one wants to purchase it from you.

How to minimize this risk:

Diversification can help you minimize this risk to a good enough extent. For example, index investing can be a good alternative, where risk is diversified over the various stocks held within the portfolio. Consider ETFs such as the SPDR S&P 500 ETF (SPY) and the Vanguard Total Stock Market ETF, which offer such benefits.

Market risk

Market risk arises when the market turns against or ignores your investment. It also happens when stock market bubbles and crashes occur, which are extreme examples of what could go wrong in the financial markets. Unfortunately, this kind of risk is out of your control and can't be resolved through diversification, as with liquidity risk.

How to minimize this risk:

My best advice is to hedge your investments by taking a counter or offsetting position in a related security. For example, if you have a portfolio of losing and moderately volatile stocks, you can purchase an inverse ETF to protect against a market decline. The inverse ETF is designed to perform the opposite of the index it tracks, so in other words, if S&P 500 index increases by 5%, the inverse S&P 500 ETF will simultaneously lose 5% of its value. By combining your portfolio with the inverse ETF, any losses on your portfolio will be offset by gains in the ETF.

So even though market risk affects the entire stock market, the extent to which the market feels the impact can be minimized. Dividend exchange-traded funds such as the iShares Dividend (DVY) or the

Vanguard High Dividend Yield EFT are also great options to help you reduce this risk.

Economic risk

Economic risk arises whenever the market goes bust for whatever reason. And we know the market can go wrong anytime, so you always want to invest cautiously.

How to minimize this risk:

The simplest way is to add bonds to your portfolio as early on in your investment journey as possible. The founder of Essex Financial Services, John Rafal, claims that a 60%-40% stock-bond mix will produce average annual gains equal to 75% stock portfolio with half the volatility, so that might be a good rule of thumb to apply for yourself. Increasing your position in good, stable companies can also be an excellent solution to riding out these downturns. And, if the problem is domestic, consider getting into foreign stocks, which are known to work when the U.S. market needs to perform better.

Beginner Strategies That Will Make You a Better Investor.

Getting started as a stock investor can bring much excitement as you think about how bright your financial future will be as you gain more control of your earning power. It can also be overwhelming and confusing because of all the new lingo and the never-ending information you're expected to learn. Then comes the challenge of executing everything you learn, where many newbies get stuck. How does one know which is the right strategy to implement? The simple answer is that you don't. There is no one-size-fits-all, and the only way you can figure out which plan to go for will be a combination of how well you know your personality, how well you understand each of the strategy options, and what your current finances allow you to do. Top that with some common sense, and you'll be ready. While I can't tell you with certainty which strategy to use, I can at least simplify the main processes we all tend to use so you can see if any resonate with you. If you pick one and realize it's wrong, don't punish yourself by sticking with it. Switching to a new strategy should be relatively easy if you do things right. One of the things I like about investing strategies is that they offer much flexibility. Of course, take your time to pick the right one from the get-go to avoid the trouble of having to redo the entire process. Regarding stock investing strategies, the main ones are value investing, growth investing, dollar-cost averaging, and momentum investing.

Growth Investing

Growth investing is often considered the yin strategy because it's the opposite of value investing, which you'll learn about shortly. With growth investing, you're investing in stocks based on the intrinsic value of a company and its potential to grow in the future. As a growth investor, you should focus on young companies demonstrating their potential for significant, above-average growth and performance. Before deciding on a company, you must ensure it indicates real signs of growth and substantial or rapid profit and business growth.

A growth investor is often looking for "the next big thing," not recklessly or based on mere speculation, but rather through intensive evaluation of a company's current health and future earning potential and how that will impact the stock. So how do you go about identifying a growth opportunity to invest in? Simple. Look at the company's recent history. Is it growing? Is the stock value increasing? The company must have a consistent trend of strong earnings and revenue, implying the capacity to deliver on your growth expectations.

One of the downsides of using this strategy as a newbie is that, more likely than not, your chosen company will not pay dividends and bonuses. The reason is that companies in growth mode need capital to sustain expansion, which leaves very little for bonus payments to shareholders.

Tools to help you become a growth investor.

Use these five parameters to evaluate the company you wish to invest in:

1. Make sure the company has demonstrated a history of above-average earnings.
2. Check if the company's forward earnings growth or anticipated earnings for the next quarter match your expectations.
3. Make sure they effectively control costs while simultaneously boosting revenue.
4. Determine how likely they are to double asset value within five years.
5. Determine the current style of oversight deployed by management.

It would be best to equip yourself with specific financial metrics to become an influential growth investor. These include understanding profit margin, earnings per share (EPS), and your return on equity (ROE).

Value Investing

If growth investing is the yin, value investing is the yang in the investing strategy world. The value investing strategy is about getting the best deal at a discount. It's when you buy stocks from companies that the marketplace has undervalued. When I say a stock is undervalued, I mean that an analysis of its financial statements indicates that the price the stock is trading at is lower than it should be. That's usually based on the company's intrinsic value. As a value investor, you're. Therefore, a bargain shopper seeks to take advantage of the irrationality you realize exists in the marketplace. Warren Buffet is considered the ultimate value investor and is known to dig into his research for years before he's ready to invest in a company. But once he's ready, he goes all in. Buffet once said, "The market is a popularity contest in the short term. In the long term, the market is a weighing machine." When he's evaluating a deal, the main concern is the true potential and stability of a company. Buffet doesn't just look at the underlying price tag assigned by the market to individual company stock shares. Instead, he studies the whole company.

You don't have to do painstaking research to find a good deal, though, or what Buffest calls "on-sale" stocks. Various mutual funds and value index companies already do the legwork and allow investors to purchase undervalued stocks. The most important thing to remember is that you must invest in the long run. Just like Warren Buffet, when you decide to buy a deal, it's got to be a long-term commitment; otherwise, it won't work. And you should also only value-invest in stocks from reliable companies, not "unknowns."

Tools to help you become a value investor.

The price-earnings ratio (P/E) is one of the primary tools used by value investors to identify undervalued or "cheap" stocks quickly. To get the P/E ratio, you must divide a stock's share price by its earnings per share (EPS). A lower P/E ratio indicates you're paying less per $1 of current earnings, which is precisely what you should be looking for.

Many experts, however, will tell you this calculation needs more to identify a good deal. So, what can you do to ensure you're not being lured into a contract by false numbers? Researchers and experts suggest we use quantitative approaches to detect distortions like combining formulaic value with momentum, quality, and profitability measures. Of course, this is stepping into the advanced stuff, so don't worry if that feels a bit out of your wheelhouse for now. Start with the basics, and as you continue to educate yourself and do a lot more market and company analysis, using these approaches will feel manageable.

Fusing Value and Growth as A Strategy

No rule prevents you from devising a fusion between growth and value investing in creating your yin and yang combination. Warren Buffet has successfully demonstrated that it can be done. Historically, value stocks are companies in cyclical industries, primarily made up of businesses producing goods and services on which people use their discretionary income. A good example is the airline industry. People will fly more when the business cycle is on an uptrend because they have more discretionary income and fly less when it swings downward because they have less discretionary income. So, you'll notice that value stocks perform well during economic recovery and prosperity but fall behind when a bull market is sustained for a prolonged period.

Growth stocks, on the other hand, tend to perform better when interest rates drop and a company's earnings take off. Typically, you'll find that the stocks of such a company will continue to rise even in the late stages of a long-term bull market, but when the economy slows down, these stocks will take a beating. So, when creating your fusion, having growth and value investing will allow you to enjoy higher returns while reducing a substantial amount of risk. By investing in both strategies, you should be able to generate optimal earnings during virtually any economic cycle. Fluctuations in returns will likely balance out in your favor over time. If this sounds like something you can handle, then master both strategies and get to work.

Momentum Investing

If you believe winners keep winning and losers keep losing, you have the right mindset to implement a momentum investing strategy. This strategy is about riding the wave and going with the flow of the trends.

In most cases, investors that prefer this strategy tend to be technical analysts because doing this right requires a lot of data and pattern recognition. We'll talk more about technical analysis later.

In essence, this is a concept that defies conventional wisdom. Instead of the usual buy low and sell high philosophy, this strategy adopts a buy high and sell higher mentality. It's based on the notion that you can earn long-term profits by riding stock while on a good run and then selling them once they've had a long bad stretch. From everything I've researched and even after speaking to experts on this topic, I still can't give you a definite answer as to why it works. All I can tell you is that it works - sometimes. And when it doesn't take momentum, investors suffer significant losses if they don't short-sell properly. Momentum investing doesn't work in every market environment, and momentum stocks are subject to shard reversals that can leave investors badly bruised.

If you use this strategy, be prepared to put in much work because it will take time, energy, and skills to research which stocks have been on a good run and still need to. For this to be accurate, you need specific complex technical indicators that tell you when to buy and sell a security.

Tools to help you.

As a newbie, if you want to test out this strategy without putting in all that technical work, you can start in a general way by looking at the trends and riding the ones that are rising. When the market is doing well, ride the wave. When it drops, stay away.

You can also follow the MSCI USA Momentum Index or the SPDR Russell 1000 Momentum Focus because such ETFs can help you use a momentum investing strategy without selecting individual securities.

Dollar-Cost Averaging

This is one of my preferred strategies; you'll see why in a minute. Dollar-cost averaging is an excellent alternative for investors who don't want to or cannot afford to invest in a lump sum. With dollar-cost averaging (DCA), you're making regular investments in the market over time. For example, instead of investing $10,000 in a single transaction, you could invest $1000 monthly over ten months. Stock prices may go up or down during those ten months, but you constantly invest the same amount, and in the end, you'll have bought more stock when the prices fell at any given month and fewer units if or when the rates were higher. It's a great strategy to help avoid the overwhelm of trying to get "timing" right when investing.

It is not mutually exclusive to the other strategies I explained, which means you can execute whatever system you choose. Let's use the $10,000 example again. With DCA, you can put $1000 in an investment account every month to help you discipline your investment habits, and you could even automate the entire process.

This strategy enables you to spread out your stock purchases. That way, you can buy at regular intervals and in roughly equal amounts, so it helps smoothen out your purchase price over time and ensures you're not dumping all your money in at a high point for prices. It can be mighty in a bear market where you can "buy the dips" or purchase stock at low points when most investors are too afraid to buy. But here's the thing. It would help if you were committed and logical about this. Your emotions must be checked because you'll often need to act when the market or a stock is down.

I consider this one of the wisest forms of investing. This strategy not only helps you build wealth over time, but it's also a good way of neutralizing short-term volatility. This is especially true for newbie investors or people who cannot make a significant investment. If you have a 401(K) plan, you're probably already doing this or can have the option to do it.

To help you become a good DCA investor.

First, you need to decide on the total amount to be invested. Next, you need to determine the window of time during which the investments will be made, and lastly, select how frequently you'll make purchases.

Once you've identified your strategy (figuring out what's most suited to your needs, personality, and desires), it's time to go forward and start practicing. As you grow in mastery and expand your portfolio, you might realize it's time to add a new strategy or combine some of the ones we discussed. Feel free to shake things up a bit when that happens.

What Is Dividend Investing

In the simplest form, this is when you invest in stocks that pay a dividend, as we mentioned earlier. Dividend investing is great for new investors looking to generate steady income or build wealth by reinvesting dividend payments. By using dividend investing as your approach, you would only look for companies that can pay you a bonus. In doing so, you create a steady stream of passive income generated by the predictable income from regular dividend payments and the capital appreciation that happens over time. Dividend investing is a safe way of investing without too much risk and with a guaranteed return. The best advice I can give you is to make sure you buy great companies and avoid getting caught in chasing big dividends.

How to find dividend companies

The easiest way to find good companies to invest in is by setting parameters based on risk tolerance and objectives. There are no rigid rules here, but I will offer a few pointers that can help. First, I want you to look for healthy companies that generate free cash from operating activities, preferably those in development, i.e., increasing revenues and profits. Make a long list of these on a spreadsheet to start with.

I encourage you to look at the historical dividends and assess the chances of them being repeated in the next few years. Consider sorting companies in descending dividend yield and gradually discard those issuers who need to be promising to maintain historical results soon.

Next, I want you to prioritize companies with a clearly defined dividend policy, meaning the company declares that they will pay a specific amount of a particular part of net profit to shareholders yearly.

The other thing I want you to do is to dig deeper by going beyond "historical records" because playing in the stock market means you value the future but look to the past to make educated choices on which way to go for the best returns. Therefore, even though historical data does help inform you, it's wise to research these companies even more. I advise selecting companies for your portfolio after publishing the results for their third quarter. You can easily extrapolate the annual impact of most companies on this basis and estimate the potential dividend for the past year. With the knowledge of the current price, you can then calculate the future expected dividend yield. I also want you to study the company's balance sheet, including debt, cash, other assets and liabilities, and the industry the business is in. Is the company at risk from competitors? Is there a strong demand for their products or services? All this research will enable you to avoid the pitfall of choosing the wrong company, even if the yield and historical records look appealing.

Metrics to Help You Evaluate Dividend Stok Before Investing.

The dividend yield is the annual dividend typically represented as a stock price percentage. For example, if a company pays $2 in annual dividends, and the stock is $50 per share, the dividend yield would be 4%. (2 ÷ 50 = 1 ÷ 25 = 0.04 = 4%)

Look for companies with a higher yield, but even more critical; as I just mentioned, finding a company that can maintain the dividend payments yearly is even more critical.

Pay-out Ratio

The payout ratio is the dividend expressed as a percentage of a company's net income. Suppose a company earns $2 per share in net income and pays a $1 per share dividend, and then the pay-out ratio, in this case, is 50%.

Earnings Per Share

The earnings per share (EPS) metric helps you understand how stable a company is. As a rule of thumb, you want to focus on a company earning more than its dividends because that's the only way to be long-term sustainable. The best dividend stocks are companies that have shown the ability to regularly grow earnings per share over time because it means the company can continue to pay its dividend and potentially increase it.

Total Return

The total return is the overall performance of a stock. It combines dividends and gains or losses from a share price change. For example, if a stock rises by 10% this year and pays a 4% dividend yield, its total return is 14%, i.e. (10 + 4).

P/E Ratio

The price-to-earnings ratio is a metric to determine if a dividend stock is appropriately valued. It divides a company's share price into earnings per share.

Regarding taxes, most dividend stocks pay qualified dividends, which depend on your tax bracket. While most dividends qualify for lower rates, some are classified as ordinary dividends and are taxed at your marginal tax rate. We'll talk more about taxes and investing later in the book. I want us to move to penny stock investing, which is extremely popular today.

Penny Stock Investing

What is a penny stock? According to the SEC (Securities Exchange Commission), this is the name given to any security valued at $5 or less per share. But for the most part, it is associated with ordinary shares of small companies that trade at low prices per share - usually less than $1- allowing an investor to buy and hold thousands of claims for relatively little money. Most of these companies are relatively new, have small market capitalization, and still need to establish a track record as successful businesses, making them speculative and high-risk investments.

The best part about penny stock investing is that anyone can do it. And I mean anyone because they are so cheap and easy to invest in. They can potentially yield huge returns for you. However, they can also lose all your money. Most of the talk you might hear around penny stocks isn't penny stalk investing. Instead, it's penny stock trading. There's a fundamental difference here to note because, in terms of risk and reward, it does make a difference whether you only want to invest in them or actively trade penny stocks.

I have realized that penny stock investing is worth digging into if you want to build wealth around smaller, less liquid companies. In the same way, some entrepreneurs are not interested in owning large multimillion-dollar companies; some investors wish to have small wealth-creation opportunities. If that's you, then penny stocks might be right for you.

A key thing about making money with penny stocks that most people get wrong is the kind of stocks they buy. You want to ensure you're investing your money in the right companies.

Characteristics of penny stocks:

High risk- high reward - It makes sense. Speculate types of investments will always be risker than usual. The counterpart to a high-risk investment is the potential for high rewards within a relatively short period. And it can be a manageable risk if you're smart enough to start small.

Small-cap - meaning they are typically tied to small-capitalization markets, which tells us that most companies you'll come across will have a stock valuation of under $2 billion.

Large bid-ask spread - The difference between the asking and bid prices with penny stocks is usually big, so you need to learn how to navigate this. Where to find penny stocks: Save your time searching for penny stocks on the primary market exchanges like NYSE or Nasdaq because you can only see the best ones through OTCBB and the pink sheets. What are pink sheets? Aside from the fact that the name comes literally since it originated as printed information on pink paper, these are over-the-counter versions of big market exchanges. Each day, the National Quotation Bureau publishes a pink sheet with the bid and asks prices for penny stocks and other stocks not traded on the more extensive market exchanges. In today's digital world, brokers can access the Electronic Quotation Service to check bids and ask prices in real-time instead of relying on that traditional daily publication. That helps when it comes to faster decision-making. Look for ".PK" after the company's stock symbols to identify a penny stock. In case you're worried there won't be many companies trading in this manner, let me assure you that there are currently more than 10,000 companies available and growing. Some investors also refer to Pink Sheets as the over-the-counter (OTC) market group.

Where to buy penny stocks:

Many people looking to get started need help figuring out the best way to purchase penny stocks. I recommend going for an online rather than a live broker. In the next chapter, we're diving into the world of brokers, so more on that later. But I discourage live brokers with this type of investing because penny stocks are incredibly low priced, which means profitability is significantly reduced if you use an expensive live broker. I suggest you learn, study the craft, and get good at trading. This is one of those situations where investing and trading overlap. And the line between being an investor and a trader gets blurred because, for penny stocks to work, the long-term buy-and-hold mindset fundamental to good investing practices must be re-evaluated. Penny stock investing is one of the investment types that should be treated as a short-term investment. This is especially true if you want to increase your chances of making money. That means you need to have an interest in active trading. So, before you get too excited about penny stock investing, consider the time, energy, and resources needed to help you succeed because this will be all hands on deck. If you're wondering whether penny stocks are worth your time, let me remind you that some individuals (Timothy Sykes and many others) have shared that they made millions in profit from penny stock investing and trading. So, some penny stocks might result in losses; others might sell with little profit, and others will do well. The most important thing with penny stocks is to have a strong strategy that plays out over months so that you gain at a macro level instead of getting caught up in single wins. It's about investing in penny stocks and trading them collectively to make a profit.

How to find penny stocks to invest in:

As with all other types of investment, market research is what you need. The more you know about the companies on the Pink Sheets, the better. Start your research by sector, then the market, then individual stock. That helps you better understand competition, performance, financials, and more.

CHAPTER FIVE

The Best Online Brokers To Use

If you're serious about making money long-term and building a healthy portfolio, immediately start thinking about which broker you'll work with. Unless you're looking to go into mutual funds or using things like cash deposits and bank savings to invest, opening a brokerage account and establishing a relationship with an excellent broker should be the first order of business. That's because, with your brokerage account, you can access stocks in the stock market. And as we know, that's where the money is. So, before diving deep into brokerage accounts and stockbrokers, let's define a broker.

Who is a Stockbroker?

This person's primary job is to buy and sell stocks and shares for people who want to invest money. A broker can be a Company or an individual and usually earns by charging a commission for the services rendered when acting as a Company. A good stockbroker must be licensed by the body regulating the stock in their state. There are two broad categories of brokers. Namely, discount brokers and full-service brokers.

Full-Service Brokers

They offer a range of services, which include market research, investment advice, and retirement planning, added to a full range of investment products. This often leads to higher commission charges for their services. Some full-service brokers can charge as high as $600 per trade. You must think, "Who in their right mind would pay that much?" The truth is that a full-service broker may not be the cheapest in the market, but they may be what you need to succeed in this industry. If you're the kind of investor who needs comfort and much handholding to feel secure, then this kind of broker might be the best alternative - assuming you can afford it. Some of the benefits you would get include:

- Tax Preparation Strategies
- Opportunities to Invest in Off-Market Products.
- Retirement Planning
- Ability to Handle Unique Trade Requests
- Access to Initial Public Offerings
- Access to Exclusive and Proprietary Research Tools
- Experience.

Read that last point again because it's essential. When you're coming into the game as a complete newbie with no financial or investing experience, it does help to have a reputable company guiding you through the whole process. The only caveat you should know is that profitability will be constricted because the fees associated with these types of brokers will tend to eat up your gains. So, there's no right or wrong here. Determine your needs, the types of investments you'll be making, and the budget you can afford to spend before deciding whether to go full-service or discount.

Discount Brokers

There are many excellent discount brokers. I have used discount brokers for over a decade and have always accepted the choice. For the average investor building their wealth from scratch, this is usually the wise choice because they are more affordable and allow you the flexibility to oversee the decision-making process. This is a good thing when you want to control all the trades, but it also has its downfalls because you won't get professional advice. So, if you make a good choice, you win; when you make a poor choice, you lose. These brokers offer us the DIY (do it yourself) experience, which is great because you get to learn the ropes and dig yourself out of the trenches. Some of the best-known and most reputable brokers I can recommend include TD Ameritrade, Fidelity Investments, Charles Schwab Corp., and E-Trade. However, you can always do more research to find your favorite.

How to Choose Between a Discount and a Full-Service Option:

There's a lot to consider before making this decision. The first step is to answer these questions:

1. Do you want to go into a long-term investment or day trading plan? If you're planning on investing short-term, then a discount broker is probably the best, but if you're doing long-term investment plans, it's wise to consider full-service brokers.

2. How knowledgeable are you about the market? If you're a complete amateur, it might be worth investing in full service because getting that coaching and extra knowledgeable support will help you understand the investment world faster than going in unthinkingly.

3. What do you want to get out of your investments? Why are you investing?

4. What kind of securities are you interested in?

Now that you've answered those questions, here are questions to ask the brokers you shortlist to see who your best choice would be. What are the costs and fees associated with doing business with you? You must ensure your budget constraints align with the broker you choose. So that means you need to understand all the possible costs (hidden & extra costs) that might arise once you open your account—things like account minimums, withdrawal fees, fee structures, etc.

What kind of customer service and customer support do you provide?

What trading platforms will you have access to?

What educational materials will they offer, if any?

Should You Go for The Cheapest?

This is a question I often get because every investor is looking to make the most profit, and sometimes it seems like a good idea to go as cheap as possible with your broker. I have learned through experience that this is a more complex yes or no answer. The broker you choose can help you make a lot of money or cause you to lose a lot. Although discount brokers are more popular because they always have more affordable rates, they may need to match your investing style and needs. You may want to invest more in paying higher broker fees until you get the hang of things, then you can switch to something more affordable. Again, this will be a choice made at an individual level. Even among discount brokers, some will be cheaper or charge no commissions at all, but you should still go for that. Discount brokers are primarily suited to intermediate and advanced investors. They only work well when you take the time to educate yourself, as you're doing through this book and other materials and tools. Going for discount brokers is okay once you know what you're doing.

If I am to give you a single answer as to whether to choose the cheapest, my response would be - don't base your decision on price alone.

Do your research, and I will share with you in this chapter what you need to keep in mind as you pick your broker, but most importantly, go for a broker that helps you make the most money overall. Instead of worrying about how cheap a broker is, consider the following:

Your investment style - Are you a buy-and-hold or actively trading investor? What kind of investment will you use most of the time? Although most brokers offer a similar menu of investment options, deciding beforehand what you care about is essential. If you're primarily going to focus on stocks, ETFs, and bonds, then you want to choose a broker that offers good value. Pay extra attention to the commissions associated with your preferred investment style.

Account fees - most brokers will charge account fees, but some have better deals than others. Typical prices include annual, inactivity, trading platform subscription, research, data fees, etc. Make sure you know how much this will cost you monthly and annually.

Account minimums - Some brokers offer no account minimum, for example, Ally Invest, Merrill Edge, and TD Ameritrade. Others require a minimum initial investment of anything from $500 and up. Find out what your broker offers.

Investing Online

It can be nerve-racking to start investing online regardless of age or how much money you've saved. I want to ensure you feel less nervous and more confident about this decision. Putting your money into investments is the best way to build wealth and save for your retirement, at least here in the United States of America. Here's how to map this process out for yourself and avoid the anxiety most people get, which often leads to procrastination. First, you need to decide why you're doing this. What's the main driving ambition here? Is it for retirement? Do you want to be actively trading as an investor or build a strong portfolio over a long period? Once you know your big "Why" for becoming an investor, you can decide how much help you'll need during your first year or two. Do a self-assessment and determine your strengths and weakness to know the best decision to make when choosing Brokerage Companies. Give your money long-term goals and short-term goals. Set a reasonable deadline for each of these goals.

Educate yourself and surround yourself with the right professional advisors, mentors, and people who have achieved what you aspire to build. Continued education will be the secret sauce that enables you to keep growing and achieve your most significant financial goals.

Pick your brokerage account and a stockbroker. They will walk you through the process of opening an account, after which you can start investing in stocks and any other investment types available, depending on your financial situation and risk tolerance. Depending on how good your broker is and the services they offer you, that initial investment process can be enjoyable or quickly become a headache. You must do your due diligence before setting up a brokerage account and entering an agreement with any broker.

How Qualified Is Your Broker?

It's imperative to ensure you're dealing with a reputable broker before investing your hard-earned money. Do your homework well because there are plenty of scammers out there. Here are some ways you can check to ensure your broker is legit.

Do a Check with Professional Organizations.

You can check with professional and regulatory organizations to see where your broker stands. FINRA offers a database in their tool called Broker Check that can give you the stats on brokers and brokerages that agree to their standards. Everyone they verify will be on that list. If your broker isn't on that list, that can be okay, too, because only some are associated with FINRA (although it does help). In such a situation that what you want to do is make sure your broker meets fiduciary standards. The Securities and Exchange Commission (SEC) also has its database of registrations for the Series 65 license, which you can access through the Investment Adviser Public Disclosure page when you visit the SEC. So, find out what certifications and licenses your broker claims to have and then look them up on the appropriate sites.

Check Online

Google the broker's name and see what comes up on Google. If you come across their social media, this is a great place to visit what they are all about and what people think about their services in black and white. Many brokers and investment advisers are also required to register with their state. If your broker claims to be written, you can make a quick call to see if their information is valid and up to date.

Where to Find the Best Online Brokers.

If you want to find the best online brokers, an excellent resource to always bookmark is Investopedia. They continue to review and update the best-performing brokers as the market shifts. Some have been top-rated for years and enjoy the benefit of brand equity, which is why I include them in this book. However, I encourage keeping up to date by doing further research to see if any new ones are worthwhile. These are the most trusted and reputable brokers right now:

TD Ameritrade

TD Ameritrade is among the best options for beginners. Hence, I encourage you to visit their website first. They have $0 trade fees, $0 account minimum, and $0 annual or inactivity fees. You can get fabulous free research and a high-quality trading platform with excellent customer support.

Fidelity Investment

Fidelity Investments has a strong reputation for its mutual funds; however, it is considered one of the best and most rounded online brokers suitable for retirement investors and active traders. Fidelity offers $0 trading commissions, a $0 account minimum, and vital customer service. It has an easy-to-use platform and gives lots of research and educational materials.

TradeStation

Tradestation has $0 trade fees, a $0 account minimum, and comes with a high-quality trading platform. They also offer comprehensive research and other advanced tools to help you master your craft. This is a popular choice for stock, options, and futures investors.

Interactive Brokers

Interactive Brokers charge $0 trading fees with a $0 account minimum, and the best part is that they also offer international trade opportunities. The Lite version provides a quality trading platform and no stock-trading commissions. However, if you upgrade to the Pro version, there is an inactivity fee to pay.

Charles Schwab

Charles Schwab is excellent, whether you're a beginner or advanced. They offer $0 commissions, high-quality research, and a robust investment selection of no-transaction-fee mutual funds with low or no minimums. In addition to the basic trading capabilities offered by Charles Schwab, they also have several powerful trading platforms, all free and available to clients of all trading services.

Everything You Need To Know About Brokerage Accounts

You need a brokerage account to invest in the stock market. A brokerage account is a particular type of "account" like a bank account but different in that it enables you to buy and sell securities (e.g., bonds, mutual funds, stocks, forex, futures, etc.). Your stockbroker, whether discount or full service, should give you access to a brokerage account, and as you've seen above, many of them will allow you to set up an account with no minimum account obligations. The money you deposit into the brokerage account is what you'll use to purchase investments.

It's good to know that you fully own the brokerage account and its assets as an investor. The broker is only an intermediary between you and the investments you want to purchase.

How brokerage accounts work and how to open one:

Once you feel ready to start your investment journey and know which brokerage Company to use, it's time to open your brokerage account. Opening an account is free and easy to do online in most cases.

All the recommended brokers I shared in this chapter allow you to open your brokerage account quickly in a few minutes. Then you can fund your account by transferring money from your checking or savings account - a process that can take a few days to a week, depending on your bank. The process is similar if you already have a brokerage account and want to move to something better now that you've read this book.

Once you sign up for the new account, you can transfer money from your old one to your new brokerage account. You often won't need a large sum to open a brokerage account. Some brokers need an initial deposit, while others don't ask for anything. Please get to know the policy with your new brokerage Company so you can organize your funds and allocate them accordingly. For example, if you go for a brokerage Company that requires an initial deposit of $1000, you need to transfer more than that amount to have money to purchase investments. Your broker should be able to walk you through this entire process to ensure everything is clear and manageable. If you're asked to choose between a cash account and a margin account, I encourage you to stick with a cash account first. A cash account is self-explanatory; you put cash in and use it to purchase. A margin account allows you to borrow money from the broker to make trades. As a newbie, this is never a good idea.

Many newbies always wonder if having more than one active brokerage account is a good idea, and the answer is yes and no. Go for it if you've got the money and can handle working with different brokerage accounts. There's no limit on the number of accounts you can have or how much money you can deposit into a taxable account annually.

Should you get a brokerage account or a retirement account?

The answer to that question depends on your investment goals. A brokerage account (a taxable account) has very few rules and restrictions. Although you have no tax advantages and your investment earnings will be taxed, you can move your money as you wish and invest as much as you'd like. If your main objective is retirement investing, a retirement account is a better way to go. You can open a retirement account such as a Roth or traditional IRA, granting you tax advantages. The catch to this is that you'll have restrictions around money movement. You can only withdraw and contribute money to such an account following guidelines, which your broker should help you clearly understand—more on this topic in the tax chapter.

What to Do with Broker Recommendations The jury is still out on this topic because some feel broker recommendations work, while others fear they don't. Many studies show that broker recommendations tend to be biased because they often favor companies with high cash flows, even if it comes from investments rather than business operations. They look for high price-to-earnings ratios etc. Going by these metrics alone could sometimes lead to shortcomings. Still, once you control for other variables, you'll find that stocks rated by analysts as buys tend to outperform those placed as sales during the subsequent one to six months. So, what does this mean for you? Use the research to understand the industry and the current operating environment. Know that forecasting on smaller stocks won't be as accurate as larger ones and give more importance to recent recommendations. Anything over three months old shouldn't be used to help you make an investment decision.

CHAPTER SIX

How To Utilize Time And The 8th Wonder Of The World

Time is tricky. If you have a good relationship with it, your investments can proliferate. However, it can also work against you if you don't learn to align your ambitions with the nature of things in the stock market world. How you utilize time once you become an investor will directly impact your success. In this chapter, we want to ensure you understand a few key concepts, all related to time.

The Waiting Game

Patience is a virtue. I'm sure you've heard that statement many times throughout life, and it holds even in this journey of becoming an elite investor. The waiting game is necessary and recommended if you want to do well as an investor. But it's not just waiting for the sake of staying.

Contrary to what most newbies think, it's not about waiting for the "whole market" to crash. Instead, the waiting game is strategic and very concentrated on a few key companies you've researched and feel confident will be your best investment. So it's not about "timing the market crash"; it's about following specific companies you believe in and knowing their total value. Then patiently waiting for the opportunity to take advantage of a temporary dip, those companies experience whether it affects the entire market.

Consider someone as successful as Warren Buffet, a master money-maker. Suppose we trace his actions and behavior as an investor. In that case, we can see that his strategies are excellently executed and tend to require tremendous research, knowledge, and patience. Warren often says that the priority (when it comes to investing) is to find cheap individual companies, ensure they have solid fundamentals, and go deep with those instead of focusing on investing in the market. His approach is simple yet requires much more work than you might think. It also requires playing the waiting game. Why? Because if you do your research, make your watchlist, and gather up your funds only to realize it's not the right time to invest, what should you do? Do you still purchase even when it's not a good deal? Of course not. As Buffet said, it's got to be a "sale."

Sales fall on your lap only a few times a week hence the importance of developing patience. You must wait until the right moment to act on that purchase. Some people assume that finding the right time is about predicting the market crash. Is that even possible? Can you envision a market crash? The truth is, predicting an impact is next to impossible. We are still determining when the next crash will be and what will trigger it. What we can do, however, is be prepared to act as soon as it occurs—based on observations and personal experience, waiting for those downtimes when the market dips are some of the best opportunities for an investor to purchase something that will yield a tidy profit.

Market Timing Vs. Buy and Hold

Buy-and-hold investing is the general term we use to refer to passive investing. It's when you purchase securities to hold for a long time. Long-term (depending on whom you ask) can be anything from three to a hundred years. On the other hand, market timing is actively investing and involves actively buying and selling. In this case, you aim to enter the market at the most advantageous time and get out before any meltdown or downfall occurs. Common sense tells us that market timing is challenging, and that's true.

According to current research, long-term buy-and-hold tends to outperform market timing investing. If you're the kind of investor wondering if you must choose one or the other, I have some good news. There's a strategy that combines both market timing and buy-and-hold methods within the same portfolio. With more education and professional help, you can combine active management with passive investing to maximize your return on both.

The 8th Wonder of The World

In this context, the eighth wonder of the world refers to the concept of compound interest. That is a topic few investors under- stand, and even fewer know how to make it work in their favor. Despite all my success and experience, I must confess that this concept wasn't clear for many years. It took a while before I grasped the importance of compound interest and how to make it work. For years I was making money but not capitalizing on this truth. I wasn't compounding my wealth, which resulted in linear growth instead of the alternative that compound interest can offer. What is compound interest? According to Investopedia, compound interest is interest calculated on the initial principal and the accumulated interest of previous periods of a deposit or loan. In other words, investing money should generate more money in the form of interest! So, as you invest and earn, that earned money starts to make money for you. How powerful is that? Compounding interest takes time. This is another waiting game because you won't see much action for the first twenty years. Things start getting exciting the longer you're in the game. In other words, the longer you're invested and the more you keep reinvesting, the more money you'll make from compounding. For example, many companies offer dividend reinvestment plans allowing you to reinvest cash dividends to purchase additional shares of stock. As you reinvest in more dividend-paying shares, your investor returns compound because the increased number of claims will consistently increase future income from dividend payouts∆ assuming the dividends remain stable. In such a case, you end up with "double compounding," which, over time, becomes a substantial number.

CHAPTER SEVEN

The Psychology Of Investing And The Mindset You Need

Winners think differently. It's that simple. If you want to be a successful investor, you've got to develop the kind of

mindset that all winners have. Many people skip over a chapter like this because they feel it's too "fluffy" or unimportant when investing. After all, investing and making money in the stock market is a game of logic, analysis, research, right choices, etc. And yes, that is true. But to assume your emotions don't factor into your decision-making and money-management abilities is to set yourself up for failure. So I commend you for reading this chapter to the end and putting some of the ideas you'll learn here into motion.

Here's the truth. You will need to work hard to succeed, and you'll also need to gain experience and mastery as you grow. The knowledge you continue to gain will make a difference in your performance as an investor. However, let me assure you that nothing will hinder or catapult your success in life more than how you think. That's why you must come to terms with your current mindset.

What is your current psychological state? Are you even aware of how you think, why you react in specific ways around money, etc.? Do you know what biases or beliefs you might have that subconsciously affect your decision-making process?

Putting Your Emotions on A Leash

A lack of control over emotions such as greed, pride, fear, anxiety, or anger may negatively impact the way you invest and, more importantly, the decisions you make concerning your investments. Having the right strategy, picking the right stock, and following your plan is fantastic, but it only sometimes works perfectly. Stock market investing requires someone who can play well in less-than-ideal situations. I recently met Steve at a conference where we were both guest speakers on investing. He shared how he learned this truth the hard way. Steve has always been a numbers guy, so he figured active investing would be easy. He considered himself very logical and did everything right by the book when he first got into investing. At first, things seemed to go well. He had a strong strategy, implemented it exceptionally well, and prided himself on always picking the best stocks. He was doing great for a young investor until the first significant correction in the share market came, and he started losing money. The only problem was that Steve was in love with the security that was going downhill. The beautiful portfolio he was carefully building up in record time started falling apart, and he lost it! As he watched the value of his investment fall, fear and anxiety crept in and overwhelmed him. It clouded his judgment and his ability to act fast. His pride got in the way because his ego couldn't accept what was happening, given how "perfect" his plan was. Studies have shown that people experience more pain in losing $1 than they would feel pleasure in gaining the same amount. Steve indeed fell into that category. The sting crippled him a lot, yet instead of selling to preserve capital, he held on to losing positions, and in the end, he got wiped out. What happened to Steve? His emotions hijacked his decision-making skills.

Steve is a very rational and logical guy. He studied, researched, and analyzed the stock market for two years before investing his first dollar. After getting into the game, he was chart reading and keeping up with the daily trends. Steve knew well what to do - when to cut losses, avoid bleeding out, etc. He knew everything, and yet he did none of it. We like to assume that investing and trading are rational processes, but we forget that our emotions influence behavior. Even if, in theory, you know what to do, if you don't take the time to understand better how you think, feel, and what drives your emotions and behavior, you might end up experiencing the same disaster that Steve had. I have shared this story with you as he did with the audience at that conference, hoping you will learn from this and prioritize mastery of your emotions.

The best way to avoid being ruled by emotions is to discipline yourself. Create a rules-based approach to investing once you determine what kind of investor you are, and then be disciplined enough to follow the rules you put in place. For example, you can decide not to change asset allocation due to recent market activity or select low-cost funds to represent asset classes in the budget. You can choose to only focus on long-term investment if that feels right for you; in this case, you can form a prudent asset allocation based on that decision that allows you to maintain that portfolio through all market conditions. Here are some tips to help you take emotions out of your investment even more. Avoid getting trapped by the minutia of daily stock trading. Unless you're an active day trader, looking at the minute-by-minute changes in the stock market and price fluctuations won't serve you very much. If anything, it will only breed fear, just as it happened for Steve. As both investor and an active trader, Steve could have taken a different course of action and made other choices. This advice is especially crucial for long-term investors. Don't feel the need to keep up with daily price fluctuations. Limited check-ins will lead to increased feelings of security and improved decision-making. Don't fall in love with your stocks. The stocks won't love you back, no matter how hard you try. Yes, it's hard to swallow your pride, admit you made a wrong decision, and sell the investment, but sometimes, that's the smart move. Emotions will try to take over and cloud your judgment. You might have all the right reasons in the world, but if it's not sound to hold on, make sure you sell that investment as fast as possible.

Put a stop loss on your investment by deciding when enough is enough. Once you cross that threshold, make sure you have parameters in place to help you execute the selling of that investment before you lose everything.

Seasonal Anomalies

In everyday communication, the term anomaly refers to abnormal behavior or occurrence. In the financial markets, however, we use this term to refer to any situation whereby a security or group of securities acts contrary to the notion of EMH (efficient market hypothesis). A great example of an anomaly that's famous occurred in 1987. October 19th of that year is considered a dark day and adequately coined "Black Monday" because a sudden and largely unexpected stock market crash started in Hong Kong and penetrated Europe and the United States of America. The collision was so severe that the Dow Jones Industrial Average dropped over 22% daily. Since then, the term Black Monday has been commonly used by critics to dismantle the efficient market hypothesis. Whenever the stock market deviates from that usual behavior, an anomaly occurs. There needs to be concrete proof to logically teach what anomalies are because they come and disappear with almost no warning (as the story above just showed). Some re-appear, while others never repeat themselves. At this point, we know that most stock market anomalies are psychologically driven, and although they can be great opportunities for you as an investor, make sure they don't dictate your trading decisions. Below I will share some common anomalies you might want to look for.

January Effect

Historically, stock prices tend to increase noticeably during the month of January. Several factors could influence this phenomenon, such as many investors usually selling off their losers in December. It could also be because investors like to use year-end bonuses to purchase new investments at the start of the year. I find this anomaly more rational than the others I'm about to share because it makes sense to cut writing the loss off your taxes.

Price Reversals

There is some supportive evidence that a reversal will occur in subsequent months when stocks perform well or poorly over 12 months. So, what am I saying? Yesterday's top performers might become tomorrow's underperformers and vice versa. Although there is some logic to this, understand that since most investors expect this shift to happen, it's probably bound to become a self-fulfilling anomaly. Unfortunately, predicting when investor sentiment or other factors trigger a price reaction is complex. Still, if you've seen a consistent rise in your winners for a long time, it might be time to re-evaluate how long you want to keep them.

Neglected Company Effect

Once you've played this game for a while, you might realize that most focus is on a specific set of companies—the more prominent players. Companies with smaller or relatively low balance sheet evaluations are often neglected and lack exposure. This causes them to be undervalued by the marketplace and makes them less visible to investors.

The days of the week are one of those anomalies that doesn't make much sense, and EMH supporters hate it the most. According to available research, stocks tend to move more on Fridays than Mondays. That has created a bias toward positive market performance on Fridays. Although it is statistically accurate, please don't assume it's predictable. It's sometimes also called the weekend effect and has been documented since the early 70s. So, I recommend you refrain from buying stocks on Monday because although this phenomenon is persistent, it still needs to be something to bank on. As with all the other mentioned anomalies, let them influence when appropriate but don't base your final decision on any of them.

Keep Calm and Invest

Stock investing is only for you if you expect to become a wealthy investor while surviving any marketplace challenges. Volatility is the nature of the beast in stock market investing, and anyone who has built a healthy portfolio can tell you there will always be turbulence. For those who have only been investing for the past few years, their marketplace experience is lacking because they haven't weathered any big storms. The real test of a successful investor or trader is different from how much money they could make in the last twelve months. Instead, it's how many market crashes and downturns they have survived. Although we've had a few minor bumps (such as the end of 2018, wherein just four months, Nasdaq fell more than 23% impacting stocks like Apple, Amazon, and Netflix), none of these have been major hits. So, let me save you some Aspirin money or medical bills in advance with this solid advice: You must train yourself to stay calm and composed as an investor no matter what's going on in the marketplace. The most robust and most successful investors I know manage to keep their calm even when the market tanks. Want a few ideas to help you do the same?

Plan

This isn't rocket science. I just told you there's no way a good investor won't experience volatility. So make sure you have a contingency plan ahead of time. If you're prepared for the inevitable market crash, you'll be more robust, calmer, and capable of making the right moves. Stop obsessing about your portfolio or what the daily charts are telling you.

If you are a real stock investor (which I assume you have read this far), then you know our game is the long-term play. As such, you must limit how often you check stock charts or your portfolio when things are going awry. This is good for your mental and emotional health and finances because you'll avoid impulsive decisions.

Back Test

Trends are constantly repeating themselves. It's easy to gain perspective when you review long-term trends and other historical records because it can help you see that stock-market corrections always work themselves out in the long run.

Ground yourself in your "Why."

Simon Sinek made the concept of "start with your why" popular in the leadership space. I want you to adopt some of that thinking to your investment because you are the leader of your stock investment business. And beyond just knowing your "why," I also want you to remind yourself of it whenever you get anxious or too caught up in the game. Investing can give us such a rush and sometimes become overwhelming. Keep yourself grounded, and you'll remain calm.

Keep Investing

This might sound wild and counterintuitive to most readers. Still, the truth is that whenever there's a downturn or market correction, an excellent opportunity lurks amid that chaos. Warren Buffet told Fortune Magazine not too long ago that he's a big fan of buying more when others pull out. "The lower things go, the more I buy," said Buffet. Of course, that means you must have a sound mind, a solid long-term plan, and the right mental state to make this work. This book is already preparing you to be ready. For such opportunities, if you implement everything, you learn.

For some, even with all the knowledge and planning, it might not be a good idea to risk further when volatility is high, which brings me to my next important point. Do you know your personality, temperament, and mindset well enough to pick investment styles that work in your favor?

What Kind of Investor Are You?

Here are the various types of investors experts have identified. See if any of these traits resonate with you so you can improve your chances of winning with your investment strategies.

Automatic Investor

This type of investor cares a lot about convenience. They prefer to have everything on autopilot and take a hands-off investing approach. If this is more your type, you're looking for solutions enabling you to automatically contribute to your investment funds by directly transferring funds from your bank account on a particular day of each month. You want the ability to sit back, relax, and focus on other things as your investment efforts work in the background automatically. You can automate your investments, especially if you choose a full-service broker who will often help automate the process and align you with the best buys and strategies that match your needs and objectives.

A significant advantage of this approach is that you don't have to micro-manage or daily monitor the volatility of your investments since most of them will grow over many years. You can avoid the anxiety that most investors and traders experience. Things like compounding interest should be of great interest to you.

A disadvantage of being this type of investor is that you may need complete control of your investment portfolio. If you lose touch with where your investment funds are going and how your portfolio performs, it might harm you in the long run. That is especially true if you rebalanced your portfolio infrequently to ensure you're getting rid of the depreciating assets.

Conscientious Investor

This investor only gets involved with companies that align with their values and moral principles. It goes beyond just making money or building a portfolio. If you're this type of investor, it's more about investing in socially or environmentally responsible companies. An advantage of being a conscientious investor is your impact and influence on others and the world as you demonstrate what you stand for and who you are through the types of companies you promote and invest in.

Unfortunately, this can also create certain limitations, resulting in lower returns. But given that you're driven by impact and a particular moral code, even that limitation may not necessarily be a disadvantage in my eyes because some things are worth more than money. And if you just resonated with that notion, perhaps this is your investor type, so take time to pick your stocks and ensure the companies you invest in align with your values.

Property Investor

This type of investor is more interested in building a portfolio that deals with familiar and easy-to-control assets. They own gold, maybe even bonds, collectibles, or real estate. If you're this investor, you care about putting your money into things you understand. The idea of Wall Street and dealing with constant market volatility is highly unsettling. So, after learning in this book how stock investing works, you might opt for a different type of investment that feels more stable, such as real estate. That's why, earlier in this book, I shared the different types of assets available to you. You don't have to invest in stocks to become financially independent. I have many friends who only invest in real estate, and they've built much wealth around that.

I encourage people to follow in my footsteps and start with stocks because I've experienced first-hand the rich benefits of this type of investing. Compared to other investment types, stock investing offers excellent returns in a relatively short time, so don't just shy away from the opportunity because it's the unknown. An advantage of becoming this type of investor is that you will be exposed to less volatility than a stock investor.

The huge disadvantage is the missed opportunity of the enormous returns of stock investing. Large-cap value stocks are a relatively safe way to start your investment journey if you want to play it safe.

Bargain Investor

The bargain investor is an intriguing type. They are always searching for bargain deals, which is fun if you like that kind of hunting. And in many cases, if you know what you're doing, you can create some big wins. If you're this type of investor, then stocks that cost $1 per share appeal to you. Penny stocks are where you like to invest your time because you see the potential and enjoy watching that penny turn into a pretty profit. Of course, there's always the risk that those bargain stocks could become worthless- but you feel it's worth taking. It's about carefully assessing the P/E ratios to check the share price relative to earnings per share before picking which stock to invest in.

As we've seen with many investors who've made millions from bargain deals, a considerable advantage of this is that you can strike big. The disadvantage, however, is that these low bargain prices could easily dupe you. Sometimes the fees are trading at low prices for a good reason. If you can sort out the fakers from the real bargain deals, you should be able to do well in the long run.

Daily Dow Watcher

This type of investor is current with what's trending up or down. They are up to speed, know the current market price, know how much their portfolio is worth at any given time, continuously monitor stock charts, etc. If the market has a bad day, this type of investor immediately stresses out and might get tempted to sell out.

A significant advantage of being this type of investor is that you're always up to speed with the current trends of the marketplace. Unfortunately, keeping tabs on the market can also be a source of frustration and anxiety because the stock market is highly volatile. If you're always on your smartphone checking daily charts, you'll get stressed and discouraged and might impulsively decide to sell stock out of fear when prices drop. By the way, selling your stock when prices drop (like most people do when a market drops) is almost always one of the worst moves an investor can make. Be informed but regulate it. Check on the stock market and your investment portfolio frequently (I suggest quarterly), and you'll be more productive and profitable.

Active Trader

If you're an investor who enjoys being an active trader, following the markets daily is a good idea. Investing and trading are not synonymous because not all investors can be profitable traders, and vice versa. Investing is a long-term game, whereas trading is usually a short-term game. Few are naturally gifted at both, and even if you can balance these two, you'd still need a massive amount of continued education to be great at both. Assuming you are great at both, then things get very exciting. This is where you play for the little wins and the long-term gains. Diversification is your ally. You want to be able to time the market correctly. And remember what I said. It's not about predicting when the market will crash. Instead, it's about taking the right action and buying suitable securities at a great price point when the crash happens. When others pull out, you pull the "buy" trigger strategically. To perform optimally, you need to buy an undervalued stock for whatever reason before other investors realize it, then sell it when it's near the peak price before most investors know it's going down. This execution will require you to immerse yourself in the market and economic data, business articles, financial reports, etc. You've got to know your stuff because none of it is guesswork. Your risk appetite must be high as well.

An advantage of being this type of investor is that you can enjoy unlimited success, especially when you get the timing right. The disadvantage is the loss you can incur. Trading fees can also get expensive if your investment approach requires making many trades, so tread carefully.

Portfolio Tweaker

This type of investor isn't actively trading. However, they enjoy frequently updating and fine-tuning their portfolio by transferring funds to get the desired balance between large-cap, mid-cap, small-cap, growth, foreign, domestic, value, and bond investment categories.

An advantage of being this type of investor is that it's easier to keep track of your progress and meet your investment goals. Please do it effectively because sometimes it might hurt your overall return. A good habit to get into is to rebalance your portfolio at most twice a year, especially if you're a relatively new investor.

Company Loyalist

This type of investor is loyal to a specific brand. They go into the stock market game, knowing exactly which company they want to pour most of their money (if not all) into. Often, it's a company they work for already or a trendy brand that inspires loyalty, such as Apple, Tesla, etc. This kind of loyalty can be advantageous because if the company does well, you'll do well.

The main disadvantage I see if you're this type of investor is that you make yourself vulnerable in the marketplace because of your need for more diversification. I've mentioned this a few times in this book and often remind my students that lack of diversification is hazardous. Putting all your eggs in one basket (even if you'd take a bullet for that brand) is not a wise move as a stock investor.

The Winning Mindset

You must work on your mindset to become a successful investor and build wealth quickly. The rules of making money as a stock investor are easy to understand and, with practice, get easier to execute. The one thing that doesn't naturally occur is emotional maturity. You've got to have tremendous mental discipline and a good handle on emotions like fear, greed, laziness, and pride if you want to succeed. An expert study reports that less than 10% of investors are rich after learning the right strategies. Why do you think that is?

I'll save you some thinking time - it's primarily because most people cannot manage their emotions and have no idea how to develop a winning mindset.

How you think about stock market investing and your emotional relationship with money will make all the difference in the world. Many new investors must correct the mistake of treating stock investing as a hobby. They think of stocks in very trivial ways. Some- times it does help to see the stock market mechanically and concha- lately because it takes the emotion out of it. But instead of downplaying the stock market to protect your feelings, how about taking a different approach? I encourage you to think of yourself as part-owner of the company you invest in. By assuming that, you become focused on the things that matter. As an owner of several businesses now, I am always thinking long-term. I don't make hasty decisions and dive into more excellent details when analyzing situations. This is a habit I also bring to my investment decisions, and it has helped me tremendously.

Another mental shift I want you to make concerns how much you need to diversify. I know you've heard, "Never put your eggs in one basket," which is true. However, I also know that being over-diversified can hurt your growth. To avoid being overstretched in any one way, invest significantly in a handful of companies. Instead of a broad yet weak portfolio, consider building a narrower portfolio with a few stable investments of good companies that show excellent growth prospects. Remember, the most successful investors do their due diligence, take their time to dig deep into a company, and go with their "gut." If you've done all the necessary research and you "feel" it's a good deal - take the chance.

CHAPTER EIGHT

Technical and Fundamental Analysis of The Stock Market

There are two main disciplines that every stock investor and trader should know if they want to do well in this industry.

These are the two main methods used to study, measure, and judge market behavior. Both are essential for us to learn as stock investors as they make forecasting easier and identify trends. These studies estimate both the short-term and long-term value of the market. Given their proven reliability, you can use these two methods in almost any investment category, so it will benefit you to learn as much as you can about each of these over the coming months. What am I referring to? Technical and fundamental analysis, of course. While this book doesn't offer a complete and comprehensive course on either (for that, I recommend taking up an online course on Udemy), it will give you the basics needed to start practicing as soon as today. The better you understand and utilize technical and fundamental analysis, the easier it will be to make informed decisions as you begin investing.

What is the main objective of doing any analysis?

To determine the current price of the stock you want to invest in is reasonable. As you branch more plunging into the two methods, a few variations arise because each analysis focuses on different aspects and time length, but the bottom line always stays the same. They are tools to ensure you get into a good deal for short-term or long-term gains.

Let's dissect the main differences between Technical and Fundamental analysis to ensure everything is clear.

The Difference Between Technical and Fundamental Analysis

Fundamental analysis is a method stock investor use to evaluate a company by determining the intrinsic value of its stock. In other words, with the fundamental analysis, you would be digging into the annual and quarterly figures of the company, studying their management, competitors, and the economy trying to get at the company's actual value to determine if you want to invest your money there.

The technical analysis concerns the actual stock price or volume data and nothing else. The balance sheet of a company or how excellent the management is will bear no significance because this type of method is more concerned with identifying trading opportunities that can produce gains in the short term. So, in other words, the price action is what counts, not the underlying economics that affects the value of a company.

It's best not to ask which method is better when clarifying these two approaches (especially as newbies). Different investors will give you different answers. Some investors swear by technical analysis, while others only work with fundamental analysis. A keen investor needs to know and utilize both methods for optimum results. You may look at the difference between these two in the following way: Technical analysis is concerned with price action, which gives clues as to the stock's supply and demand dynamics in the marketplace. That determines the stock price and when it's an excellent time to buy. The focus there is price and volume data.

On the other hand, fundamental analysis concerns a company's value. It's about identifying the value of its assets and the profits it can generate. The focus is knowing the difference between a stock's underlying value and the current price at which it's trading in the marketplace. Short-term price movements are always determined by supply and demand in the market, which are, in turn, affected by more than what you'd find as you dig into the fundamental analysis. You can only analyze market sentiment and the effect of emotion on market activity through price and volume data.

On the other hand, regardless of how detailed your charts are, it's impossible to determine whether a stock is genuinely under or over-valued. And you certainly cannot forecast or predict any company's value years into the future. Hence, while charts are excellent for reflecting on what has happened in the past, they aren't that valuable when you're looking to make decisions about your future.

Tools to use for fundamental and technical analysis:

The company's financial statement is the most important data source for fundamental analysis. You need to understand the company's current financial health, such as the company's income statement, balance sheet, cash flow statements, etc. Does the company have debt? You need to know this. Have they recently changed management? That should matter to you. With all this information, you can calculate ratios and metrics that reflect the company's performance, health, and growth rates. You intend to arrive at and determine what is fair value. You can only do that by comparing several models and ratios.

Technical analysis requires charts. The main tools used in this analysis method are chart reading, including price charts (line charts, candlestick charts, bar charts, etc.) and various other indicators such as oscillators, price patterns, and complex analysis frameworks like Elliot Waves. As you can see, technical analysis is quite broad and highly complicated.

Which one should you focus on?

Again, I reiterate my statement from before. There is no right or wrong because it's not a binary answer. It depends on the type of investor you are and what your objectives are. Why would you be reading this book as an intelligent investor, which I assume you are otherwise? I will study both. Why? Because Fundamental analysis is extremely useful for long-term investments, which we said is the main game with stock investing. Technical analysis is also instrumental when doing things like market timing and short-term trading, which many of my students get into to make some money in the short term as they also build their portfolios. So, combining both is a winning strategy if you want to be an investor who is also actively trading. Therefore, instead of telling you which one is better, let me aid you in approaching this smartly.

How to Use Fundamental and Technical Analysis Together in Stock Investing

A practical implementation of what we just discussed is to start by building a watchlist of stocks you're prepared to own based on the fundamental analysis you've conducted. Once you have your list, use technical analysis to decide if or when to buy them. Next, you should look at a price chart to get an idea of the direction of a trend. This will help you determine whether the market agrees with your valuation. Have a stronger conviction when going against the crowd and be prepared to exit quickly if a stock is widely owned and the fundamentals change.

You can also use fundamental research to determine which parts of a business cycle are most profitable for a company and then use technical analysis to confirm anticipated trends.

Another way to combine both is to use technical analysis to find good entry levels for growth stocks in an uptrend. Companies with high growth rates and trade on high valuations often experience significant corrections. In such cases, your technical analysis can be used to identify oversold levels, which is an excellent opportunity to buy growth stocks.

Trading Is Better for The Short Term in The Stock Market.

Have you ever heard of day trading? It's a trendy style of trading for short-term investing that earns you money over a short period. In other words, it's fast returns and typically very liquid. It's one of the most attractive ways to make money on the Internet today and perhaps one of the main reasons you picked up this book. You can buy and sell shares through day trading, earning a profit to achieve immediate gains. And yes, anyone can become a day trader. It works by finding good deals you can quickly enter and exit to achieve a high return in the shortest timeframe possible. Sometimes you enter and exit trades within a matter of minutes. Yes, it can get intense and exciting. Your ability to exercise patience and, at the same time, be quick to act determines how well you do in any given trade. Let me be clear here. Day trading will not build your investment portfolio. It's not meant to play that game. Day trading is about earning you money, giving you a source of income in the short term if you need it, and much of that hinges on your ability to get rid of shares fast.

The price movement that continually goes up and down throughout the trading day (hour by hour) is what you're monitoring because that's where your profit lies. As you might have guessed, this game is more about psychology than numbers. Numbers play a minimal role in day trading. You need a good trading strategy that you must learn and develop to suit your personality and master; then, you must implement it religiously. There is no wiggle room, and you must follow your trading plan. That's where your mindset makes a difference. If you want to go down this path, I encourage you to further your education by studying day trading for beginners.

Investing Is Better for The Long Term in The Stock Market

The whole purpose of stock investing is to build something profitable long-term. That's where the real money is. Even though day trading makes you money, it must differ from what you can create for yourself with long-term investments. A healthy portfolio is a mix of mid to long-term investments, but as Warren Buffet evangelizes, the main aim should always be going as long as possible because that makes all the difference. Long-term investments always do well despite market fluctuations, downturns, recessions, and volatility. If you can weather the storms of the marketplace, then you will win. One of the main advantages of this type of investing is that dividends and compound interest become very attractive and plausible. We already mentioned the benefits involved in both earning rewards and being able to compound your interests. The psychology you need is also different.

When making long-term investments, you typically run a much smaller risk of losing money on the stock market, and you don't need to concern yourself much with the daily drama of the marketplace. If you choose a great broker who can offer you reasonable transaction costs and who helps you set up the correct account for your preferred investing style, you should be good to go - no stress, just a lot of patience. If you invest your money long-term, go as long as possible (preferably 20 years or more). To be confident that this will pay off in the end, use everything we've discussed in this book so far, don't shortcut your research, and above all else, go for companies you genuinely feel will appreciate over time.

Chapter Nine

How to Buy Stocks and Deal with Recession

Now that you understand how to use fundamental and technical analysis and combine them in your stock investing business, it's time to apply these lessons. Using what you've learned, you will now be able to choose the right stock, and in this chapter, I want to assist you in doing so. Afterward, I'll also share some insights to help you deal with the inevitable market downturn,

crashes, and even possible recession so that you're always prepared.

How to choose the right stock.

By now, you should realize that selecting a good stock to build your portfolio must begin with an in-depth study of the company's fundamentals. In other words, you need to become a fundamental analyst. The goal is to ensure that the stock you invest in is worthwhile. And to help you spot any red flags you need to become aware of before taking the plunge. An excellent place to start is by researching companies you already know, whether you've used them as a consumer or read about them for years in financial papers etc. By now, you should already have your brokerage account and ample know-how on implementing the fundamental and technical analysis you've learned in this book. It would be best to have an investment plan with a clear strategy. If you apply everything you've learned and have an excellent broker to assist you, picking your first stock to fit your investing needs should be easy. If your due diligence allows you to go ahead and buy the stock, decide how many shares you want to buy.

How Much Does It Cost and How Much Should You Buy

The cost of becoming a stock investor will vary significantly based on various factors, many of which we've discussed. Factors include what broker you'll choose, which type of investment style you'll go for, how many shares you'll buy etc. There are no stiff or rigid rules for investing here. You can invest as little or as much as your financial situation (and investment account) allows. The two main factors when it comes to stock price are the price of the stock itself and the fee (commission) your broker charges. A young company still in its early stages of an initial public offering (IPO) can only be purchased on the primary market and is usually set by the issuing entity. This price is fixed and non-negotiable. Suppose you want to play in the secondary market to buy a company not in the early IPO stage. In that case, the price isn't predetermined by the issuing entity or fixed, as it varies depending on the market psychology. As for the commissions, it depends on whom you work with. Some charge a flat fee; others charge a percentage of the total trade value, etc.

In some cases, there will also be other extra costs associated with having a brokerage account, so you want to consider all these things when deciding on your initial investment, but suppose you go for a reputable online broker such as TD Ameritrade. You know they charge no fees for account minimums, and opening an account is quick and easy, so you can begin your investment journey with as little as $500 and grow it as you grow. The cost of the stock you buy will also vary. If you go into penny stock trading, you can buy way more shares with a $500 investment compared to buying Netflix or Amazon shares. So, make sure your ambitions match your finances.

Buying Your First Stock

I recommend you start as small as possible. Dip your toes into the water and get a taste of what it's like to own shares before diving into the deep end of the ocean with the sharks. Instead of pouring all your money in at once to fill your entire portfolio, make your first purchase of a single share of a company you feel convinced will do well. If you have the skill, mental and emotional stability, and strength to ride through the rough patches that might arise without losing your mind, then start adding to your portfolio over time as you continue to educate yourself.

Recession and How to Take Advantage of The Situation

Nothing hurts the economy and, in turn, companies and the stock market more than a recession. A recession is a slowdown or a significant halt to the economic growth of a country. There have been numerous recessions in the past, the biggest one being the great recession that ended in 2009. That created much devastation in the marketplace as people sold off their assets in panic. While it can be devastating to find yourself in the middle of an economic meltdown (which no one can ever predict accurately), it's not all doom and gloom. Going through a recession can work in your favor if you don't panic and create a contingency plan. The first lesson you must learn about a recession is that it won't last forever. And once it's over, the investors that weather the storm and stay strong usually come out on top because the market always recovers after a recession.

There are a few things you can start doing whenever you notice the market is beginning to show signs of decline. You can take advantage of a declining market through the dollar-cost averaging method discussed earlier in the book. Go back and read that section if you can't recall. Another thing you can do is diversify your portfolio by purchasing dividend stocks through mutual funds or exchange-traded funds that only invest in dividend-paying companies. More on what ETFs are later.

Investing in consumer staples is the best possible strategy for surviving a recession. What are consumer staples? Think of companies like Walmart, Proctor & Gamble, etc. Even if the economy is down, families still must spend money on food supplies, medicine, hygiene products, etc. They may not buy cars, televisions, or other luxury products, but they'll undoubtedly continue to shop for necessities. The more you can invest in such companies, the better off you'll be during a market downturn.

Recently U.S.News shared an article with the seven stocks that have historically soared even during a recession. According to their report, the stocks that held up during the 2008 recession were Hasbro (HAS), Ross Stores (ROST), Walmart (WMT), Amgen (AMGN), Anheuser Busch Inbev (BUD), H&R Block (HBR), and Dollar Tree (DLTR). You're familiar with some, if not all, of these companies. In the report, we are told that when many dividend stocks were slashing to ceasing payments altogether, Walmart managed to grow its earnings per share and even increase its dividend by 8%. This leads me to my second important lesson about a recession. If you're going to hold stocks during a recession, the best ones to own are the ones that demonstrate much resilience. A company that is established and has a strong balance sheet and cash flow. I'm a huge fan of consumer staples because if you choose the right ones, you'll get a nice cushion during the crash and emerge even more significant than before, assuming you apply the right strategy.

CHAPTER TEN

The Easiest Way To Make Your Investment Strategy Passive And Grow Long-Term (Index Funds and Etfs)

There are dozens of ways to get passive income. Of course, this is every investor's dream, and regardless of how you plan on doing it, the two main elements needed to turn that dream into reality will always be time and money. You need to have time or money to make it work. Most people starting this game have neither. Suppose you've got much money already but need more time to generate passive income. But if you're starting from scratch with little or no money, you'll have to invest much time initially before you can reap the rewards later. The most vital component of creating passive income is honesty, assessing where you are, and putting in as much effort as needed without wavering until things snowball. For some, it might mean working late into the night. For others, it might mean cutting out on too many social get-togethers or binge-watching Netflix on weekends. Unless you can make the sacrifice, that dream of passive income will remain a wish.

As an investor, you can focus on being passive or active. Do you know what the difference is between these two terms? Let's clarify.

Passive Investing Vs. Active Investing

Passive investing is more about automating and being hands-off with your investments because you intend to do it for the long haul. This is the classic buy-and-hold approach, which we've discussed throughout this book. As the name implies, active investing means you're very involved in managing your portfolio. The goal is to beat the stock market's average returns and take advantage of short-term price fluctuations. Therefore, you need to be deeply immersed in technical analysis and learn to predict as much as possible market timing. You can succeed as an active investor if you can be more right than wrong. However, if you're not interested in playing that intense game of chasing the latest trends and price movements, then you'll be best taking on a passive investor role. Have someone else manage your portfolio. Passive investing is straightforward, and you always know which assets are in an index fund. The fees are low, and it's very tax efficient. A downside to this type of investing is that your returns will be low since you're not actively trying to beat the market or get the most significant profits. Passive funds are also limited to a specific index or predetermined set of investments with little to no variation.

On the other hand, active investing is flexible, and you have complete control over your portfolio and its investments. You can hedge your bets and sell off the losers to offset taxes on the big winners. One of the disadvantages of being an active investor is that the risks are much higher. It also comes with costly fees because of all the buying and selling involved, which incurs transaction fees and commissions. Over time, those fees can eat up your returns and profits to the point where it makes no sense to maintain your portfolio, so be intentional with whichever path you choose. Both styles are beneficial, but one might be more favorable depending on your personality and investing objectives. Aside from direct (single) stock investing, there are other investments you can add to your portfolio to continue building wealth. Here are three types.

Index Funds

An index fund is a mutual fund - a collection of stocks, bonds, or other types of securities that tracks a market index (e.g., S&P 500). Before you can understand what an index fund is, you need to understand the definition of an index.

According to my knowledge, the word index is a made-up concept. An academic idea that's been accepted by the masses and the marketplace. It's a person or a committee sitting down and creating a list of rules for constructing a portfolio of individual holdings. For example, one of the oldest index funds is the Dow Jones Industrial Average, a list of thirty blue chip stocks selected by The Wall Street Journal editors. The list comprises a representative collection of stocks that are important to the economy of the United States, and they are weighted based on the stock price. Instead of having a portfolio manager making selections with an index fund, you outsource the capital allocation job to the individual or committee determining the index methodology.

How do they work?

Index funds are managed by fund managers who make sure the fund tracks the underlying index. They can be structured in two primary ways: Index mutual funds (offered directly through mutual fund companies) and index exchange-traded funds (these trade now on stock exchanges). If you own index exchange-traded funds with your brokerage account, you can easily buy or sell shares at any point when the stock market is open for trading.

Exchange-Traded Funds (ETF)

An exchange-traded fund is a basket of securities you can buy and sell through your brokerage Company on a stock exchange. This can be stocks, bonds, commodities, or a combination. ETFs have become extremely popular because they have the diversification benefits mutual funds offer while simultaneously mimicking the ease with which stocks are traded. You can buy market ETFs that track a particular index like the S&P 500, bond ETFs, commodity ETFs that track the price of commodities such as oil, gold, or corn, foreign market ETFs, Inverse ETFs designed to profit from a decline in the underlying market or index and so much more.

How does it work?

ETFs work like a company stock during the day when the stock exchanges are open. An ETF has a ticker symbol, and intraday price data is readily accessible during trading. The number of shares outstanding in an ETF can change daily (unlike a company stock), and this is due to the continuous creation of new shares and the redemption of existing shares. The market price of ETFs generally stays in line with their underlying securities because of the ETF's ability to issue and redeem shares continuously. ETFs are popular with investors because you can buy and sell them any time of the day, you have better control over capital gains tax, and because they are traded like stocks, you can place various orders. The fees are also relatively low as there is no sales load. You only need to worry about the regular commission to your broker.

As with all investments, some drawbacks come with investing in ETFs, including technical issues while tracking an underlying index. This can create unfortunate discrepancies. Some thinly traded ETFs also have a wide bid/ask spread, which means you might buy high and sell low. If you invest in small amounts regularly, there may be better solutions than this, as there are other lower-cost alternatives for investing directly with a fund company in a no-load fund.

Dividend Investing

If you have been reading this book looking for a proven system to help you build wealth primarily through passive income generation and were wondering when I would spill the beans - this is it right here. I have seen this method work for myself and countless others. This is the surest investing strategy that can create a passive income but can be challenging. It can be done.

Dividend investing, which we discussed in an earlier chapter, is very straightforward. The only thing you need to make this system work for you is a good understanding of what dividend investing is and how it works, and you need the mindset to execute. That means you must be patient because dividends only work if you use a long-term approach. You need to invest in companies that pay dividends. Start with one or as many as your finances permit, then add to your portfolio as your income grows. When you receive your payout, don't just spend it on stuff. Instead, it would be best to reinvest it to purchase more shares to build a profitable and secure portfolio in the long haul (more than ten years later). Let me repeat - the main objective is to buy shares that pay dividends and hold on to them as long as possible. It is a long-term investment that earns you money as the years roll on.

What about diversification?

Diversifying your investments is always a good idea, and it's no different here. I recommend purchasing from other companies and even sectors whenever possible.

CHAPTER ELEVEN

Tax Protected Investments

There's a lot to learn when you're getting started on your investing journey, and most of the time, we tend to neglect the topic of taxes, mainly because of how overwhelming and confusing the issue is. So, it's understandable if you feel tempted to skip over this chapter. However, I encourage you to resist that temptation because understanding how taxes work will save you many headaches. Death and taxes are inevitable; you've heard that saying. I encourage you to avoid death at all costs. But regarding taxes, a little knowledge on how to best manage will prove wise for your peace of mind and wealth-building efforts.

Tax System On Your Investments

You can only grow your stock investments if you understand the tax basics on ordinary income, capital gains, and capital losses because these affect your investment strategy. The most important thing to know as a new investor is that here in the United States, you only pay taxes on investments that increase in value if you sell them. Also, the holding period matters when calculating capital gains taxes because long-term investments are subject to lower tax rates.

Ordinary income

Ordinary income investment profit is taxed at the same rate as wages. Depending on your tax bracket, you can calculate how much tax you need to pay. The two types of investments that fall into this category are dividends and short-term capital gains. So, if your tax bracket is 28%, then that's the rate at which your dividends and short-term capital gains will be taxed. For tips, some exceptions occur depending on whether they happen in a tax-sheltered plan such as a 401(K) or an IRA and whether they fall under the "qualified dividends" type, a dividend receiving preferential tax treatment. Be sure to check with your accountant for exactly what applies to you.

Regarding short-term capital gains, this applies to stocks you've sold for a profit (that you owned for a year or less). To calculate whether the stock falls into this category, you must use the trade date (date of execution), not the settlement date. Again, even with this scenario, you might be exempt from taxes if the gains occur in a tax-sheltered plan.

Long-term capital gains

This occurs when you sell an investment at a profit you've held for over a year. The gains are taxed according to the IRS's long-term capital gains tax rates depending on your total taxable income (0%, 15%, 20%). In addition, if you fall into the category of the higher-income taxpayer, you might also have to pay a 3.8% net investment income tax, which applies to any investment income (e.g., interest income, rental income from real estate, dividends, etc.) In short, long-term capital gains receive more favorable tax treatment. Also, they offer different ways to manage and control your tax burden. A conversation with your accountant and financial planner should help you understand your income bracket and the advantages available to you.

How To Pay Lower Taxes on Stocks

The easiest way to do this is by thinking long-term instead of short-term. Consider holding an asset for at least a year, preferably more, as that will qualify you for a long-term capital gains tax rate when you sell. As mentioned, long-term capital gains taxes are much lower than short-term capital gains taxes. You might pay less tax on your dividends by holding the shares long enough for the rewards to count as qualified dividends. This doesn't mean solely focusing on the long-term. Be intentional about the stocks you buy and the type of account you open to ensure everything aligns with your investment goals and works in your favor.

There are two types of investment accounts. Depending on your choice, you will be exposed to certain drawbacks and advantages regarding taxation. The two models are taxable accounts and tax-advantaged accounts. In this book, we've primarily focused on a taxable account (a brokerage account is a taxable account). Taxable accounts are outstanding because they have more flexibility, offer few restrictions, and you can withdraw your money anytime for any reason with no penalty or tax. However, they have no tax benefits. Tax advantage accounts such as a 401(k) or an IRA are usually tax-exempt or tax-deferred. However, you do pay taxes when you withdraw your money, and you also don't have the flexibility or freedom to move your money as you like because they come with specific fixed rules. For example, in 2020, you can contribute $6000 to your IRAs or $7000 if you're 50 or older. With a 401(k), you can contribute up to $19,500 or up to $26,000 if you're 50 or older. It's great that you don't get taxed upfront with such accounts. It is wise to hold all your investments in a tax-advantaged account. Still, given the limitations, I need help finding it efficient. That's why I've focused purely on a brokerage account.

Depending on your investment goals, you need to figure out what the best solution will be. A good rule of thumb when deciding what would be the "right account" is to keep those investments that lose less of their returns to taxes on a taxable account. Then the ones that could lose a lot of the profit on taxes, I suggest putting those into a tax-advantaged account.

How To Protect Your Investments

The best way to protect your investment is to educate yourself on money management and get a qualified accountant who can assist you in understanding your tax situation because it will be different for everyone. Then I encourage you to contact a taxable and tax-advantaged account, as most intelligent investors have both. Allocate the right assets to the preferred accounts (as suggested in the last paragraph). For example, I would put individual stocks I plan to hold for longer than a year into a brokerage account and wait for them to qualify for long-term capital gains. Then individual stocks meant for the short term (less than a year) would go right into my IRA or 401 (k). In other words, whenever I actively manage stock funds that generate short capital gains, my go-to account would be the tax-advantaged one. Then as I diversify and grow my portfolio with index funds, ETFs, etc., those would mainly be on my taxable account. Makes sense? The more you can minimize your taxes, the better off you'll be. Everyone will have a unique situation depending on their income bracket, whether you apply as a single or married couple, etc. So, this is meant to give you only some of the details you need, but it does give you an overview and a starting point in this often-overwhelming topic. Now, make an appointment to see a qualified financial advisor or tax professional so you can choose the best tax strategy for your goals and current situation.

CHAPTER TWELVE

Investing Your Way to Complete Financial Freedom and Early Retirement

If you want to achieve financial freedom and build enough want to achieve financial freedom and build enough wealth that enables you to retire whenever you desire, you've got to make it happen. It takes effort, a lot of intention, commitment, and discipline most people aren't willing to deploy. Having read this far, you're different from most people. You are determined to design and live your life on your terms. It's a very noble decision, and you sure deserve it. So let me be honest with you. The way to achieve complete financial freedom and early retirement is to learn these three things:

First, you need to get good at making money. That includes your current job or business and the investments you will make in the stock market.

Second, you need a plan to help you keep this money. You can only save money when you know how to manage, budget, and make it work for you, which leads me to my last tip.

Third, you need to know how to multiply your well-managed money so it can go to work for you and make you wealthy.

If you can focus on those three key steps, you will find yourself in that elite club of financially independent men and women who get to travel the world, do what they love, and live life on their terms. I assume you're already good at making money and earning an income. This book has just introduced you to the best way to take your current cash and use it to build wealth. But it wouldn't be a complete book if I didn't help you think through the plan of how you'll make your investments work for you. To do that, let's talk about your investment plan.

Creating an Investing Budget

If you want financial freedom and early retirement to become a reality, you must set the right goals. It would be best to have short, intermediate, and long-term goals leading to that bigger picture.

With your short-term goals, you want to think about and embrace having a tight budget that you always live by. Then you want to start planning an emergency fund. These are relatively easy things to do if you stay disciplined and committed. For your budget, you need the following:

- Non-discretionary expenses. These include rent, insurance, water, gas, food, clothing, transportation, etc.
- Discretionary. These include luxury items, vacations, gifts, sports tickets, social outings and eating out, etc.

Once you understand how you're spending your money and where you can make cuts or put spending limits, you can decide what percentage of that income will go into an emergency fund and stock investing. Next, it will be time to set up an emergency fund. This is the money you set aside to pay for unexpected expenses. I would start with a goal of $1000, and then once you hit it, you can expand it. Having a retirement fund is also good, but this one should be a top priority because it will become the foundation for the financial stability you need to achieve complete freedom. Now that this is in progress, it's time to consider mid-term goals. For your mid-term goals, it's time to start thinking about life insurance and disability income insurance. If you're young and have student loans to pay off, focus on that first. This is also where you can consider buying your first or vacation home. A dream car, dream home, or college for your children also falls into this category. When you have your list, determine how much you need to start making and saving to move in that direction.

For your long-term goals, think about the future and how you want life to be. For most people, that vision is retirement with enough money to travel the world, a big home, and enough money in the bank to live a comfortable lifestyle. Visualize your future, allow yourself to dream, and then estimate what that will cost. Do you want to own two houses? Do you want an apartment in the South of France? What is that lifestyle for you, and how much will it cost? A little Google research can help you determine some numbers to help you figure out the expenses. Then with some simple math and assistance from your financial planner, you should know precisely how much money you should save each year to move toward that dream. Once you have a complete (or relatively clear) picture of your financial plan, making an investment plan becomes easy. Why? Because now you understand your objectives, and you know where you stand.

Depending on your current financial situation and goals and how much you are willing to invest, your broker will advise you on the best investments to get started. If you have a small investment budget, you might need to start small, which I always recommend, and things like Penny Stock Investing, ETFs, etc., might be the best way to go. Refrain from assuming; ask for professional advice not from a friend or family member but from a qualified investment or financial advisor.

How To Save More Money Easily

Even as you focus on investing and wealth creation, saving money is essential. The more money you save, the more you'll have to invest, advancing your wealth creation efforts. Remember what I said earlier? Two main elements needed to build wealth are time and money. Creating more time may not be possible, but you can generate more cash through savings. With those savings, you can reinvest, buy more significant stocks, and diversify your portfolio even more. Here are a few ideas to help you get started.

Pay off credit cards in full each month. That will discipline you to spend only what you know you can afford, and it will shave off those high-interest rates.

Stop impulse or "sales" shopping. You'd be surprised how much money you'll save if you stop buying things because they are on sale or discounted. If you don't need it and it's not making you money - don't buy it.

Brown, bag your lunch to work. If you spend $5 per day for lunch, yet homemade lunch made the night before would only cost you $1.50, then in a year, you'd have saved an extra $840 ($1200 - $360). That's an emergency fund, and you still get some money left over to give yourself a treat.

Stay away from getting rich quick schemes and fads. This is such a money waste for many investors. Please stop giving money to someone who promises a magic bullet or shortcut to get rich. There's no such thing! Stick to tried and true investments and only invest in what you know.

Don't go cheap on your broker and accountant. You'll waste way more money if you choose the wrong broker and financial advisor because they are more affordable. So, save money in the long run by selecting reputable companies and individuals to support, advise, and guide you on this journey. Stop eating out and clubbing every weekend. As long as you spend money on bottles and pay for dinners every weekend to impress people, you'll struggle to grow your wealth. If you don't need to eat out, stay home and cook a healthy meal. Spending money, you don't have to impress people who don't even matter, wastes time and money that you could pour into investment opportunities.

Cancel your subscriptions. It may not seem like much money but add up how much it costs you to have all those streaming apps for sports, movies, entertainment, and other unnecessary software apps that you probably need to remember why you signed up for. You'll soon realize it's a lot. You don't have to cancel everything, but you don't need Netflix, Amazon Prime, Hulu, etc., all at once.

Tips for Making More Money

While saving money and paying off your debt is prudent and wise, learning how to make more money is equally important. We must learn how to make money outside of a regular day job. It's not a class taught in any school (even business school). So, if you're thinking, "I need a way to make more money to fast-track my investment journey," this will help.

Creating a Business

Many individuals have started a start-up or a side hustle and turned it into a giant profit-making machine. Mainly thanks to the Internet, ordinary people like you and me who had nothing have created businesses that turned them into millionaires. You can do the same with little to no money.

Purchasing a Business

Why start something from scratch when you can purchase a turnkey solution and start operating for profit almost immediately? If you know what you're doing and get a good deal, purchasing a business can instantly amplify your net worth and enable you to make huge strides toward your financial freedom. Facebook bought Instagram about a year after its inception. While it seemed like they paid money for it then, it's worth less than the billion Zuckerberg initially paid.

Commodities

Beyond stock investing, you can also build your wealth quickly and more safely, according to most experts, by trading commodities. It's a diversification strategy used by many experienced investors. They use it for long-term investing or to park cash during bearish markets. Entities include precious metals, energy, agricultural produce, and even unique collectibles. Just because most people don't see it as risky and volatile as individual stocks doesn't mean it's risk-free, so make sure you know what you're getting into.

Real Estate and Properties

This is one of the oldest forms of wealth creation. Oprah has often been quoted stating that she loves buying houses like most women love shoes. I don't think she believes them just for fun (although she probably has fun doing it). Real estate investing is less liquid and more cumbersome, but it's one of the least risky ways to make your money work for you. Regardless of the market fluctuations, people will always need a roof over their heads. If you choose the right kind of real estate, that is wealth appreciation that you can bank on.

These are just a few ways to make money and catapult yourself into a future of complete financial freedom and early retirement. Take it one step at a time, invest your time, money, and resources in what you know and resonate with, then expect to reap the rich rewards of your hard work as the years roll on.

Afterword

You made it to the end of this book, and that's a tangible demonstration that you are committed to making this financial dream a reality. In summary, I want to remind you of key concepts as you begin your investment journey. Depending on your personality, risk tolerance, and wealth objectives, you must understand what kind of investor you want to become. Once you know your identity, you can easily play to your strengths and become a more passive or active investor. This will also help you determine your financial goals, investment goals, and what kind of broker to choose.

The next important step is to outline your budget, create an emergency fund, and set some money aside as your capital for investing. Learn about the marketplace (the stock exchanges) and the right ones to research the stocks you'll buy. Take your time with this learning process because the more due diligence you do, the better you'll be once you purchase the stock. If you're going to do penny stock investing, remember that game doesn't happen in the primary markets, and you're better off mastering the process so you can DIY the process and save your profits. If you go for the big players, make sure your fundamental and technical analysis is on point because you'll be throwing money away with these skills and a solid strategy. We've outlined how to pick the right stocks, where to find them, and use metrics such as price-earnings ratio, dividend yield, earnings per share, etc., so implement everything you've learned before making that first purchase.

Investment education and the right mindset will make a difference in this journey. I need help to iterate the importance of continued education and continually working on your relationship with money. Your emotions and psychological state could make or break you in this game.

To become an elite investor and carve out your financial future, you must surround yourself with experts and educational materials to help you become fluent in investments before real exponential growth occurs. That doesn't mean you become a passive consumer and never actually act. Instead, it means you take time to learn as much as possible. Perhaps even Δ you get started the right way and avoid the overwhelm and frustration most newbies usually experience.

Investing and financial freedom processes. Keep learning, experimenting, and acting consistently, and you'll soon be living the life of your dreams.

BOOK #2

Passive Stock Investing for Beginners

A Comprehensive Guide to Stock Market Investing, Unlocking Financial Success in The Best Way Through Disciplined Passive Investing

Introduction

So, you have, for some reason, decided to invest in the stock market, or at least, you're now thinking about it. Perhaps you heard the success story of someone who invested in the stock market or saw it on TV or elsewhere. Whatever your reasons are (and they are essential), they've led you to this little book to help you get where you want to be.

Investment is a necessary part of life; everybody is investing something into another thing. Investments work on the principle of delayed gratification. In other words, it involves you paying something right now in the hope that it will produce more substantial dividends in the future. For example, a young man that decides to eat healthier is investing in his health. He is settling in the hope that he will reap some benefits in the future, such as a healthier and better life. Thus, we can see that investing is a significant part of life. Why don't most people understand the Stock Market and its workings?

Like any other thing in modern times, the entire system of Stocks, the stock market, and investments have become so complex that it's easy to feel that you need to be some professional or guru to succeed at investing in the stock market.

Good news, you don't. While the steps and services of an expert in the industry, like a broker or a brokerage, you can still do well-selling stocks as you are. How? That's what this book is about.

I created this fantastic guide for beginners who wish to invest in the stock market but do not know how to go about it. You, like many others, probably do not know much, if anything, about the stock market. You don't know what strategies to use or even what a P/E ratio is. That's why I've put this book in your hands. With a little application and dedication and this excellent little book, you'll understand precisely what the stock market is about, why you should invest in it, and every other thing you'll need to know to become successful at trading stocks.

In this book, I present Stock Trading in straightforward terms; the entire concept of stock and why investing in stocks is sensible. I then show you case studies of those who have spent time trading the stock market, become experts at it, and are wealthy along the way. It doesn't matter why you are approaching the stock market, whether it's to build a nice little nest egg for yourself and your family, increase your family's status, or perhaps you are looking to build capital for your business. Whatever your reason, investing in the stock market makes these dreams possible.

One thing that we will look at quite early is why exactly you are trading. Contrary to many people's opinions, people invest in the stock market for various reasons, and that alone will dictate how your investment should and could be managed. Understanding yourself, your needs, and your goals as you invest helps you set realistic goals and approach the market with the right frame of mind.

Before we even get deep into stock market investing and the strategies you should employ, we'll examine the crucial subject of risk. This is one subject that every participant in the stock market must understand, novice or not. How much trouble are you taking on, and what is the potential reward ratio? If one thing causes problems for stock market investors, it is not managing their risks well. Fortunately, I talk extensively about risks and how to handle them properly. You don't want to be that guy who is too shy and always misses opportunities. At the same time, you do not want to be the guy that jumps on every bandwagon and buys any stocks you can get your hands on until you get into trouble. Just keep this in mind as you go forward.

"High Risk, High Reward, Low risk, Low Reward."

Now, there might be a question in your mind, why should you listen to me? I've been investing in the stock market for years and have profited considerably. I have also been a teacher to countless other people in different situations. I've helped them excel along the journey and even surpass their goals. Of course, with my experience, I realize there is no "one-size-fits-all" approach to help people start with Stock Marketing. Why? Because people are different. Their motivations, learning styles, and thinking patterns all differ.

Hence, you'll have to eventually work on it to get an investment system ideally suited to you. Whatever you think you do or don't know, you'll agree with me that there is a profit to be made by trading stocks. Stocks are an excellent way to increase your profit margins. For example, if you bought $1,000 worth of stock on Netflix in 2007, it will have been worth over $50,000 in 2017. An investment of the same amount in Apple will have netted you about $12,000 within ten years. Yes, these kinds of profits are indeed possible. However, the question is, how do you know the best companies to invest in nowadays? Let me explain a bit further. The whole concept of a stock is to buy a share in a company, then as the company's value increases, your stock grows and becomes more valuable. While this is probably an oversimplification, it's perfect for now. So, the challenge remains, how do you identify the companies of the future? This is because, for a single success story, many companies probably flopped, folded up, and lost value.

However, this book examines how to identify value stocks and killer opportunities and how to take advantage of them. We'll look at exactly how to identify and value stocks and how and what to avoid when trading. We will also look at the investment strategy you must implement to reach your desired goals as soon as possible. Along the journey, we'll examine some of the most excellent stock market investment strategies that some of the best investors have used successfully for years.

Granted, the strategies in this book will take time to make you rich. However, you will learn the essential things, how to keep your money and avoid buying stocks in companies headed for the rocks. In other words, you have my word that by following the strategies and instructions in this book, you will increase your portfolio slowly and steadily, and after looking back in a few years, you'll be shocked at how far you've come. I cannot give you arbitrary numbers and percentages of the profits that you will make. Your success as a stock market investor largely depends on you. Your willingness, determination, and consistency in applying what you've learned will determine how far you'll go as an investor in the stock market. This book is as comprehensive as possible, and as such, I can promise that if you read it, understand, and follow the strategies in this book, you'll learn to avoid the common pitfalls that occur many a stock market investor and well, that makes you much better than any run of the mill investor, and puts you at a higher chance of first NOT losing all your investment and, of course, making a tidy sum of profit from your investments.

Plus, it would be best to understand that you miss out on the wonders of compound interest every day you don't invest in a day. For example, if you invest 7.5% annually, a $10,000 initial investment will grow to $20,000 in 10 years, then $42,000 in the next ten years. After 40 years of steady growth, that $10,000 will have grown into $180,000. Your investment will snowball in the later years because of compound interest. So, investing sooner rather than later is in your best interest. Plus, this is the era of startups. If you can purchase stock in a great company, your profit margin can grow expo-mentally.

Finally, I can say with absolute certainty that the strategies I share in this book are real-life ones that I have used personally, seen others use, and helped others to make an unbelievable amount of returns on the stock market. (Of course, this depends on you putting the work in). Each chapter of the book will outline what you need to do in simple, straightforward, and easy-to-understand language to apply what you've learned to start making a profit. With every chapter you use, you move closer to gaining financial freedom and living your desired life.

Ready? Fasten your seatbelts, open your mind, and come with me on a journey into Stock Market Investing.

CHAPTER ONE

Why You Should Invest In The Stock Market

At some point in your life, you probably will have some money saved and start thinking, "I probably should invest this into something." You can't live in this modern age and be deaf to the oft-repeated advice of the way that leads to financial freedom.

Save and Invest

That advice is solid. If you are going to be free financially and accessible early, you will have to diversify your income or at least find a way of using money to make more money. Money is simply an asset but a depreciating asset. In other words, due to inflation, your money will lose value steadily and progressively.

Money and Inflation

Here's what I mean. If you dug into the ground, hid $1000 way back in 1960, and then dug it up in 2016, you'd have lost about $7,000. Why? The answer is inflation. Generally, money loses value the longer it is kept. What does this mean for you? It means you'll need more money in the future than you'll need today, even if your expenses do not increase.

The rate at which your money loses value depends on the inflation rate, and since 2000, the inflation rate annually is between 1% and 4%. That means your money loses value by about 1% to 4% annually. This is the issue with many 'safe' investment options. The interest rate will probably earn you enough for your money to retain the same value. In 2018, for instance, the inflation rate in the United States was 2.4%, and the best 'safe' investment you'd probably have found online was a 6-year CD from a commercial bank, offering 2.7% per year. Plus, there's no assurance that the inflation rate wouldn't have increased to 3% or even more. If you've saved up enough money to buy a Toyota, then keep the money under your mattress for about 20 or 30 years, then when you.

Take it out. It'll probably be enough to buy a bicycle. Invest it with your local bank In a Certificate of Deposit, and then, in 30 years, it'll still be able to buy you a Toyota. Invest in the stock market, however, and you can probably get a Maserati or something fancier. That is why investing is a no-brainer. While saving is a good strategy for managing your money in the short term, you need a plan for investing for a long time.

Why You Should Save

Ok, I know you've seen this everywhere. Everybody, at one time or the other, has been asked to save. If you are reading a book on the stock market and how to get into it, you probably already have a saving habit, or if you don't, you at least know why you should save.

Saving is a good strategy for anybody. No matter who you are, what you do, or how much you earn, saving a percentage of whatever you make is good practice. Many systems have been proposed, from keeping the biblical tithe to an 80-10-10 model. You spend 80% of what you earn, use 10% to pay off debts, or give to charity, whichever works for you, and save the final 10%. There are other versions of these systems, including some ruthless ones. I remember reading somewhere that you should save 60% of your income. Hey, whatever floats your boat!

My primary concern, however, isn't that you should save; instead, it is on what you do with that money. Depending on how much you earn and your responsibilities, you can have $1000 and more saved up per annum. The thing is, as good as savings are, they are still dependent on active income. You can only save from what you earn, and if you only save money for a long time, eventually, you will stop working, then what happens then? That is why I believe in investments and the power of interest. In other words, don't stop at setting some money aside. While it is a good idea, saving and storing it will eventually make it useless if you don't invest it.

Did you need more convincing? Let's look at something the great Albert Einstein described as the 8th wonder of the world and how it applies to your money.

The Wonders of Compound Interest

The stock market is an excellent place to invest your Money. You could make a tidy sum if you take it slow and steady and invest intelligently. The wonders of stock market investing become apparent when you do a little math with compound interest. What is compound interest? It is interest that is added to the claim that you already have.

Let me break it down for you. In the case of simple Interest, if you invest $1000, and the interest rate is 10% per annum, then the same interest will be the same yearly. That means that in the first year, you'll get interest of $100, the same in the second year and the same in the third year, and so on. At the end of 5 years, you'll have $1,500 as your investments + interest. With compound interest, however, at the end of the first year, you'll get $100 as interest, with $1,100 after the first year. In the second year, however, the 10% interest is calculated on the $1100 that you now have, so the interest of the 2nd year will now be 10% of $1100, giving you the interest of $110, so the total you get at the end of the 2nd year is $1,210. You do the same for the 3rd year, the 4th, the 5th, and so on. At the end of the 5th year, you'd have $1,610.51 as your investment + interest.

I know this probably looks small, but let's consider another scenario. If you have $10,000 saved up and then invest it at a rate of 7%, which is an average gain rate for investments in the stock market, then you will have $20,000 in 10 years. That means you'll ignore your original $10,000 and another $10,000 you made from investing. What's better, this is passive income. You don't need to leave your job to be able to get it. Instead, it grows and matures independently (of course, provided you did your homework well and invested smartly).

The incredible power of compound interest made Albert Einstein call it the world's eighth wonder. He famously said compound interest was the "eighth wonder of the world, and that he under- stands it earns, and he that doesn't pay for it." Compound interest does not seem like much when you start small, but leave it to accumulate over time, and you'll be amazed at how lucrative it can be.

Investing in the stock market helps you tap into this incredible power. Going by our earlier example, if you are a prudent saver and can save up to $10,000 per year and then invest it into the stock market every year, you can do that for 30 years. You will have invested $300,000 in the market. If you invested smartly, didn't take too many risks, and the world didn't end, then at the end of that 30 years, guess how much you'll have received as profit? A whopping $710,730. In other words, in 30 years, an investment of $10,000 per year will be worth over a million dollars. If the stock market can help ordinary people become financially free, why don't more people invest in it?

What You Need to Know About the Stock Market

In the late 1990s, investment was the new craze; everybody was investing in something, whether established companies, .com businesses, or real estate. Estimates say that about 50% of Americans invested in one thing or another around this time. However, many investors became wary of investing with the crash of the .com bubble in the early 2000s, the real estate crises in 2000, and the stock market crash in 2008. Just do a Google search of "Should I invest in stocks" and see an overwhelming number of results that tell you no. While it is true that the stock market may not be everything, I genuinely believe that anybody can invest and make money from it if they are willing to do the work. Throughout these crashes, many investors have realized they must become knowledgeable about their investment instead of leaving it to the "so-called experts." It makes no sense to me that you will invest your hard-earned money in a business without learning about what you are investing in and how the market works. Granted, you will not become an expert broker, but with the abundance of knowledge available today, you owe it to yourself and your future to learn about the stock market and how it works. I'm not talking about going to study to become a broker; instead, I'm talking about giving your attention and time to material like this book you are reading to attending investment meetups so that you can become a more confident investor. Historically, stocks have earned more than any other form of investment for their investors. According to the records, investors in the US Profited the most by buying stocks than any different kind of investment option.

Another advantage of investing in the stock market is its simplicity. With the advent of the Internet, you can trade remotely and buy stock from a broker with a few clicks. Of course, you should ensure that you do market research on each store that you buy from. Remember, you must be able to learn to understand the stock market, how it works, and how to profit from it.

Stock Market Strategies

In this book, you'll not see many rules; instead, you'll find it full of case studies, suggestions, and explanations. That is because there is no real hard and fast rule to how you invest. There are simply some basic principles that you need to follow, as well as some background information that will serve you well. Generally, however, in my years of investing and helping others invest in stocks, here are some basic lessons that I've learned.

Buy Stocks when they are rising in price rather than falling. And when buying more stocks, you should only buy them when the price has risen higher than the original purchase price, not when it drops below it. You should purchase supplies when they are nearer to the annual high. Don't buy when the stock has sunk so low that it looks cheap. It would help if you purchased relatively higher-priced stocks than lower-priced ones. Also, learn to sell stocks with a little loss rather than just waiting to recoup losses with the stock bouncing back. Maybe taking this loss is the best gain you can make for your overall percentage gain in inventories.

When studying the companies that you want to invest in, you should pay less attention to the book value, dividends, and PE ratios (don't worry, we'll cover all these shortly) – The last 100 years have shown that they aren't as indicative of progress s they sound. These indices do not point to America's most successful businesses. Instead, it would help if you focused on factors that have reliably been shown to reflect the real success of a company, such as the rate of profit growth, the price, and volume action. You should also consider if the company is a profit leader in its industry and how superior its products are.

While analysis and breakdowns from "experts" are valuable, you don't want to base your entire investment strategy on them. Don't allow these reports and recommendations to influence you overly. After all, analysts wrote them who are expressing their opinions could very well be wrong. Lastly, make charts your best friend. Numbers never lie, and if you're going to be successful as an investor, you must be able to read and interpret the information provided by graphs. Coincidentally, all these actions run contrary to our fundamental human nature. We love to jump on the bandwagon when things are going well and jump off when things aren't. The reality is that the stock market, like any other market, is simply a theatre where human nature and crowd psychology are put on display. The laws of supply and demand also play a part here too.

A study of the chart patterns today reflects the same things they did 50 or even 100 years ago. Although the players have changed, the game and the rule haven't. Understanding the principles that have driven the stock market's success for 100s of years will allow you to build up your portfolio and invest smartly and sensibly to build a great future. By studying the chart patterns of the stock market success stories, you can identify better stocks and companies to invest in and help you run far away from the ones that look promising but are doomed for failure.

Voices in the Market

There are a million and one voices in the market today in the form of books, research papers, expert websites, and blogs that seemingly have the "best" advice on investing in the stock market. The direction can sometimes be opposite and yet be proven to have worked for proponents of each strategy. My aim isn't to be another voice in the market but to show you a way.

Remember, I assume you are holding this book and don't know Jack about the stock market or investing in it, so I wrote this book to give your insight into the world of stocks. Also, I will explain some of the basic principles that guide the stock market and then describe with case studies what strategies have worked and why they did. As you read this book, you will find among these strategies the one that suits you the best and allows you to express yourself in the best way. There are many paths to success here, and my job is not to sell you my course but to show you how to find your path.

As I stated earlier, there isn't a one-size-fits-all approach to investing; only one way is the best for you and how to find it.

The Rock Stars of Investments

Stock market investors come in many shapes and sizes, but some prolific individuals have made extraordinary success by investing. The most exciting thing is that many of these industry leaders have varying views on approaching the market, yet all succeeded as investors. Success in investing is not about the path taken but the journey itself. Let's look at some success stories from investors and see what they have to say. And if you haven't done so yet, find books, blogs, or any articles written by these folks, as it will help you make even more money in Stocks.

Ben Graham

Ben Graham was a successful investment manager and an excellent finance teacher. Among his contribution to the industry were two classics on investments still in use today. He is also recognized for fathering two fundamental disciplines in acquisition – value investing and security analysis.

The essence of value investing is that any single investment must be worth substantially more than the investor must pay. He was an ardent believer in fundamental analysis. He consistently invested in companies that had solid balance sheets or companies with little to no debts, profit margins that were above average, and healthy cash flow.

John Templeton

He was one of the 20th-century contrarians and was said he "bought low in the Depression, sold high during the Internet boom, and made many good calls in between." He created some of the world's most significant and successful investment funds internationally. He later sold his Templeton funds to Franklin Group in 1992. In 1999, Money Magazine described him as "*arguably the greatest stock picker of the century.*" He was eventually knighted for his many accomplishments.

Thomas Rowe Price, Jr.

He is considered the father of "growth investing." He was formed in the struggle with the Depression, and he learned not to stay out of stocks but, instead, to embrace them. He was a crowd-opposer, with views contrary to his days. In his opinion, he saw financial markets as operating on a cycle and believed in investing long-term in good companies. While this is a popular opinion today, it was virtually unheard of in his days. His philosophy was that investors should focus on picking individual stocks on a long-term basis. He rose to success on the wings of discipline, consistency, process, and fundamental research.

John Neff

John joined Wellington Management Co. in 1964 and stayed with them for over 30 years, managing 3 of their funds then. He preferred to invest in industries that were popular via indirect paths. Neff was considered a value investor, as he focused on companies with low P/E ratios and high dividends yielded. He also managed the Windsor Fund for over 30 years, which ended in 1995, with a record return of 13.7%, more significant than the S&P 500 for that same period. In other words, the fund made a gain of 55 times the initial investment made in 1964.

Jesse Livermore

Livermore needed formal training in stock trading or even formal education. He was a trader who learned from both his wins and losses. Many successes and failures cemented the trading ideas you can still find today. He began trading early, in his teenage years, and by fifteen, had reportedly produced profits of $1,000 and above, which was serious money in his days.

Peter Lynch

He managed the Fidelity Magellan Fund from 1977 to 1990, in which their assets skyrocketed to $14 billion from $20 million. More importantly, it was recorded that Lynch repeatedly beat the S&P 500 index benchmark for 11 of those 13 years, with an average return of 29% annually.

He was often described as a chameleon who adapted to whatever investment style worked at that time. However, when picking specific stocks, he stuck to what he knew or could readily understand.

Warren Buffet

Last on the list is the Oracle of Omaha. He is considered one of the most successful investors in the history of investing. A follower of Benjamin Graham's principles, he built a multi-billion-dollar fortune mainly by buying stocks and companies through Berkshire Hathaway. To compare his success, an investment of $10,000 in Berkshire Hathaway in 1965 will be worth more than $50 million today. Buffet's investing style is disciplined, patient, and value driven. All traits that have seen him outperform the market and emerge as one of the wealthiest men in the world.

Now that we've looked at a few successes, you can see that their success wasn't tied to a single strategy. Instead, their understanding of the market, patience, and commitment to a process that worked for them made all the difference. And as you step out into the world of stock market investing, doing the same will make and keep you successful.

CHAPTER TWO

The Fundamentals To Understand

In straightforward terms, investment is laying out money now with the expectation of receiving more money in the future. At Berkshire, it was more comprehensively described as forgoing consumption now to have the ability to consume more later. Investment is, in other words, a consideration of tomorrow while living today. It is like the agricultural concept of sowing in winter and reaping in summer or the proverbial idea of "making hay while the sun shines." You invest in your hay days to enjoy your gray years better. It is a means to a successful and fruitful end.

Here, you will learn that:

- Investment is committing money somewhere, hoping for a later return or profit.
- Unlike instant resource consumption, it sets money aside for the future to grow.
- It is a life risk, and it is a probable loss.
- Stock market investment offers the best investment experience to beginners.

As investors, we will learn how to maximize returns and profits while minimizing costs and possible losses.

What is the Nature of your Investment?

Before opening any online broker like Fidelity, etc., somebody will question you on the kind of investment you are open to and the level of risk you can take, hence the question; what kind of investor are you? Before you give your money away, you must answer these questions because it will translate to the value of your money.

Some individual investors are open to putting the money out there in the spirit of "I hope it comes out good," while others are up to track and follow up on the progress of their investment. **Online Brokers**

There are full-service brokers and discount brokers. The former provides exclusive financial advisory services on various sectors of their investor's lives, they charge significantly as a result, and the high-net-worth owners populate their clients. While discount brokers provide tools for picking your transaction choice, most advocate the set-in-and-forget-it offer. Subsequently, online brokers have updated their services in this century with educative resources on the Internet and mobile apps. Though some brokers are without deposit restrictions, investors might be challenged with other limitations and charges to the unlimited deposit accounts. Before investing, one must keep this in mind.

Robo-advisor:

The goal is to utilize technology to reduce investor costs and streamline investment advice. The robot advisor resulted after the 2008 crisis in finance. *Betterment* is often reputed to be the first; after its launch, other robot companies have come up, like *Charles Schwab.* If you want an algorithm to evaluate and make decisions for your investment, including tax-loss investment and rebalancing, that is what the robot advisor was made for. A long-term wealth builder or an intending long-term investor will need it for investment analysis.

Investing Via Your Employer

For someone on a tight budget or a not so high- income earner, invest as low as 1% of your income through your employer. This is deducted before taxes are, straight from your paycheck. A 1% into your retirement plan will likely not hurt so much, and subsequently, with adaptation and management, you could increase the percentage and add up your investment.

Minimum Amount to Create an Account

Most institutes offering financial services have a minimum level for deposits. Some companies might not even proceed with your application with less than $1,000 readily available for a warranty. You can cross-check for the best viable option to suit your budget plan. And you should view and examine the brokers' reviews. Some firms do not require a minimum deposit amount; others have lower management and trading fees costs, while others might offer free commissions on specific terms and conditions.

Commissions and Fees

Economically, trades are on give and take, and nothing goes for nothing. Everything comes with a price. Some brokers might be racing to provide little or no commissions, but they are not charity organizations and must make it by other means. With low commissions on trade for investors, which incentivizes existing and potential investors, the brokers still must make it up.

Majorly, brokers give charges for trading stocks, the fees ranging from as low as 2% to 10%. While 2% might look like a minute amount, your profitability depends on your trading frequency and investment amount.

For instance, if you have a $2,000 investment and want to buy five different stocks, they are viewed as various trades and charged individually. The fee is 2%, which will make up 10%. On purchasing the five stocks. Your $2000 will be short of $200 already, leaving you with an amount of $1800.

If you decide to sell these stocks again since that is what investment is all about, you will lose the same amount, and in the end, you are at a 20% loss from your initial investment amount just by buying and selling stocks. If you intend to be a frequent stock trader, check the cost-friendly brokers before investing.

Mutual Funds Load (Fees)

Apart from the fees of buying mutual funds, there are other charges to be incurred, including the Management Expenses Ratio (MER), which is charged by the management team and ranges from 0.05% to 0.7% annually. It is diverse according to the funds involved. Fortunately, a high MER earns an equally high investment charge.

In mutual funds purchases, several sales charges are termed "loads": front-end, no-end, and back-end loads. These deserve extra checks to avoid future unexplained additional charges. For beginner investors, mutual fund fees are an advantage because all you need to do is meet the requirements of owning an account, and you can invest as low as $50 monthly in a mutual fund. This is known as Dollar Cost Averaging (DCA).

Reducing Risks by Diversifying

Diversifying means separating your investments to avoid a crash. It is wise not to put your eggs in one basket. Investing in several assets cannot all fail simultaneously, allowing you to stay on top of your game instead of losing it all when one investment fails.

However, as earlier discussed, this has a downturn in trading fees and losses, so for a not-so-large investment fund, you should start up with just two companies at most. Mutual funds and ETFs tend to have more diverse companies and assets within them, making it easy to diversify, and this is an advantage for their investors.

As a beginner investor, you must.

- be up to date with your limitations and available restrictions.
- find out the minimum deposit restrictions available and compare commissions.
- then, the choice of which broker to engage in business with is yours.

What are Stock Fundamentals?

Frequently on investment shows and talks, analysts, executives, fund managers, and investors alike use the word "fundamentals" or about which stock has solid fundamentals and how to build strong fundamentals. Well, opinions vary as others think it needs to be emphasized and more critical. However, what are "fundamentals"?

They are a critical analysis of data, charts, and other terms apart from the primarily focused trading patterns, which may improve the value of the stock. It is technically starting from the basics of the store to build up exceptional value.

It is aimed at a company image, identifying the fundamental value of shares, purchasing based on the information, and so on, as opposed to the "technical analysis," which is all about trading, prices, history, and records. The following are pointers to access the fundamentals of a company:

- Cash Flow
- Assets Return
- Conservative Gearing
- History of Retaining Profits for Future Funding

- Capital Management Soundness for Maximization of Profit and Returns.

Think of a stock market as a trading mall with various goods in diverse categories. Suppose the consumption rate (as in purchase) of gadgets inflates, and the consumers seem to be headed for all the Huawei gadgets. In that case, this will be picked up by a technical analyst and a fundamental analyst. A technical analyst will move with the crowd and aid the purchase by making Huawei gadgets available in surplus, hoping for an increase in price due to demand-pull inflation. However, a fundamental analyst is more profound and product-oriented than a customer-oriented one.

As far as they are concerned, customers are emotionally expressive individuals who cannot be trusted for a balance regarding the actual value of products. The fundamentalists wait for the crowd to clear and then give a situational analysis of the gadgets' scrap value, internal ware, and hardware. This is like an evaluation of value, like a book review. They will focus on the quality of the Huawei gadgets, their functions, portability, battery durability, processor speed, storage capacity, and every other target for value to get the customer's review.

Ultimately, he comes up with an intrinsic value of the gadget that is not dependent on the current price. If the sale price is worth their inherent value, they move on to purchase and, if otherwise, not. Fundamentals with a good deal do not equal profit. It takes work to be a fundamental analyst taking time to evaluate a company's intrinsic value and long-term returns. But this can save an investor the trouble of loss or future uncertainties and fluctuations in investment. A total view of a company does not translate to profit in the long run because investors may run out of luck with delays when the market tides fall. So, investors must be assertive in their investments and investment inquiries.

For a confident investment, there is much that the investor can do to learn and train on the fundamental analysis to identify a stock with solid fundamentals, and they become better stock pickers.

Major Stock Market Terminologies

The stock market is a significant advantage associated with a free market economy by providing stocks, shares, and corporate bonds for individuals to buy. It engages regular investors in sharing companies' profits, earning returns, and making profits through capital gains and dividends, although the risk of losses is not eliminated. These are achieved in many financial ways and services made available.

Price to Earnings Ratio:

This is the ratio of share prices over the annual net income of the firm per each of the shares. It is like the cost of producing a jar of milk relative to the revenue or profit made from the production. A high rate of Price to Earnings Ratio (P.E ratio) indicates increased demand for the product. And otherwise. This ratio is calculated in the number of years to earn enough to pay back the original purchase price. It could also be estimated with proposed estimations of the following year's earnings per share in the denominator. The simple formula is; Price/Earnings per share (EPS) =Price to Earnings Ratio (P.E ratio).

Price to Sales Ratio

This is derived by dividing the per-share stock price by the per-share revenue. It is a metric for valuing stocks and how much investors are willing to pay per dollar for a store, and it is usually done over a Trailing Twelve Months (TTM). Price Sales ratio is most helpful in comparing similar sectors because of industry variance. It is also mainly used for nonprofit organizations because of the limitations that sales may only sometimes reveal the complete picture. Price Sales ratio compares a company's stock price to its revenue over time.

Book Value

This would be the accumulative worth of a company in cash if somebody liquidated its assets with every liability paid for. It is merely the value left of a company after its liabilities and depreciation have been deducted.

Formula: total assets - intangible assets - liabilities = Book value. Deriving a company's book value is nothing tactical, as it is already present in the balance sheets and as "shareholder's equity." For example, if the balance sheets for Cadbury Limited report $365 million as total assets and about $285 million worth of liability, the book value (shareholder's equity) is $80 million.

Meanwhile, Market Value - or Market Cap - refers to the price a company is worth or rated in the market. It is the total value of a company translated into dollar amounts. It is calculated in the units of Current Market Price (CMP). Formula; Market value= company's outstanding shares - CMP.

Book value is significant because, as the intrinsic net value of the company, it serves as a tool for the investors to decide if a company is over or underpriced.

Why Should I Invest?

Individuals who do not invest have no financial life support. You are on eat-as-you-earn, which is much riskier than it is with the risk of loss while investing. Here are reasons why you should invest your money and assets.

- **Money Growth:** investment wagons like stocks, bonds, and deposit certificates offer returns for your investment, which increases your money and allows a gradual build. It aids wealth and asset creation and growth.
- **Save for Retirement:** as I said earlier, investment is living

minimally today to have plenty tomorrow. It is wise to save while you work, make your savings into investments like real estate businesses, stocks, bonds, and mutual funds, and at retirement, when there are no longer any steady earnings, you can comfortably live off your life savings and investment. At a young age, one is prone to taking risks; the lower the chances, the better. However, the risk is less when you are young because it's easy to learn from experience, and you have more time to invest. So now is the time to invest.

- **Attainment of financial goals:** Investment aids the achievement of big dreams at a faster rate. Because the interest is more in value and speed than just savings accounts, these investments, when matured, can be used to pursue big dreams like purchasing a big house, a lake house, a business startup, and other seen, foreseen, and unforeseen goals.

- **Increased returns:** As discussed earlier, for a high return, you need to invest in a high place that can offer high returns. You must invest big to save big and get equally significant returns.

- **A chance to get employer's matching programs:** Employers sometimes put it out there for those who invest in a 401k plan to help them top their savings up to a certain amount. And one must meet the stated amount to qualify for this matching.

- **Support others:** Most investors like to invest in people. Apart from the value of land, which does not diminish, next to it is human value. So, investing in humans and being a support system might take time, but it makes such people satisfied and content. However, long-term support means investing rather than living now and paying later.

- **Beating inflation:** It is a known fact that investors gain during inflation. Instead of spending the money you earn just as it comes or trying to save by stuffing your pillows and mattresses, making investments in bonds, buying shares, and so on, prove productive in times of economic instability like inflation.

- **Employing your money:** Most people - if not all - are employed for the salary and financial benefits they hope to get, and they work hard for the latter. Meanwhile, as an investor, you make money work for you and make a twist to the general rules. You invest your money, and without hard work, your money grows, and yields increase. For instance, if I invest as little as $50 at an annual interest rate of 7% over the next 30 years, in the end, I will have made over $350 without lifting a finger.

CHAPTER THREE

How To Get Started Buying And Selling Stocks (And Save On Fees)

You know the legal term of arbitration, where one guy serves as a medium between two conflicting parties. The arbitrator is not a party to any side but a neutral person who stands in the middle-level ground to resolve a conflict for a price or an agreed pay from both parties. This is different from litigation, where each party has an advocate who stands in defense. The arbitrator is the BROKER, driving this analogy down to the stocks and investments business world, while the litigation advocate can be an AGENT. And they are not the same because one is neutral, whereas the latter must be either white or black and in support of their employer. However, our discussion is targeted at BROKERS. According to Wikipedia, a broker is a person or firm who arranges transactions between a buyer and a seller for a commission when the deal is executed. A broker who acts as a buyer or seller will be referred to as a 'principal' party to the agreement. Brokers, in a nutshell, are the individuals or firms who stage for purchase between two willing parties, and, in the end, they get their cut or percentage profit from the transaction based on the initially agreed rate or mode of payment.

Brokerage Fees

This is the amount a broker gets for successfully staging a purchase. It is the compensation a broker receives as a reward from any transaction, usually based on the value of a percentage of the transaction price.

Workability of Brokerage Fees

Take, for instance, Rowland, an entrepreneur who wants to purchase 250 shares in the ADX group of companies at the rate of $50 per share. Whereas the brokerage rate is at 2%, the cost of the transaction will result in; 250 × $30 = $7500. $7500 × .02 = $150. $7500 + $150 = 7650.

After a while, you might resell the shares, which will require the same brokerage fee except if otherwise stated or agreed upon. And at this rate, the investor's transaction will be primarily affected in terms of returns and initial value. The investor will run at a loss, especially with frequent buying and reselling of stocks (changing positions) that only require a little capital. Also, some brokerage firms will charge maintenance and other fees, increasing investor expenses. Knowing the result and making decisions accordingly would help if you made yourself aware of these charges.

However, the deal of brokerage fees depends on the type of broker you invest in. Some full-service brokers provide everything, including trading information, research materials, etc. In contrast, Discount brokers concentrate on the former is more expensive to execute the trade and hardly anything else. The fees go further to gain on the investment size, the number and size of businesses, and the customer's account.

Investors need to evaluate their preferences and the fee structure before choosing a broker to deal with, to avoid a broker that significantly upsets the investor's plan to save money. There are many brokers, so finding a suitable one for your preferred plan should not be difficult.

Best Online Brokers

Online Brokers give you viable access to investment products and packages like bonds, mutual funds, stocks, and ETFs straight out of your mobile smartphone or devices. With the various kinds and brands of brokers online, finding the best might be challenging. Still, according to Investopedia, the brokerages shown below are the best brokers to use based on information collected through user reviews.

- Fidelity Investment
- TD Ameritrade
- Charles Schwab
- Interactive traders
- E*Trade

We will describe them here, showing the pros and cons.

Fidelity Investment:

They offer tools, services, and value, whereas updates and upgrading are ongoing.

Pros:

- Improvement for stock and options trade
- Access to active Trade Pro for all customers
- Low and comprehensive fees

Cons;

- Multiple platforms are needed to access all of their tools.
- The account operation is restricted to only.

- U.S. citizens and residents.

TD Ameritrade:

Pros;

- Availability of exclusive tools and materials
- Novice investors are made comfortable with the educational material offered.
- Channels have been made like, Facebook, Twitter, and so on.

Cons;

- Difficulty in researching because of too much content in the system.
- Multiple trading systems to find the necessary tools

Charles Schwab:

They offer complete services and technology to everyone, that is, self-skilled traders and financial guidance seekers. They also provide full banking capacities and, thus, many other exclusive platforms.

Pros;

- Refund for unhappy or unsatisfied customers
- Mobile web platforms and native mobile apps for functionality.

Cons

- It takes effort to achieve the most desirable features.
- Push towards using financial advisors, which may make them lose confidence in their abilities.

Interactive brokers:

Pros;

- Prices are on the low end.
- A gearing platform for highly active traders
- Excellent analysis features.

Cons:

- Small accounts are subject to fees.
- Education is only offered if they support education accounts.

E* Trade:

Pros;

- Streaming strategy options
- Availability of tools to future traders
- Use of performance risk tools

Cons;

- High level of margin rates
- There is no bank integration.
- There are other listed best brokers, which include:

Robinhood: This broker is best known for the free trade of stocks, unlimited and permanent. It gives access to free options trade and cryptocurrency trades.

Ally Invest: This low-cost brokerage attracts bulk discounts with more trades. It was formerly known as Traducing until 2016. Ally purchased it, and it is beginner friendly. It gives competitive standard pricing even in foreign currencies.

Merrill Edge: this brokerage is taken from Merrill Lynch, a street powerhouse that failed and got sold out in 2008 to the Bank of America. Its primary unique feature is the involvement with the Bank of America rewards program, so for a customer of Bank of America, it is perfect for complying with that account. These brokers have diverse brokerage fees, values, and individual uniqueness, which an investor should consider more carefully while picking any of them, as evaluating available value and preference is necessary when considering investing.

Considerations for Choosing an Online Broker

As a potential investor, you must think and evaluate your needs at that moment and in the most immediate future. Are you a beginner? If so, are you interested in a direct investment or one with educational materials? What is your budget amount for investment? What brokers offer an unlimited deposit for investments? Are you always on the go and a fundamental Internet user? What brokers have incredible mobile apps? How accessible and reliable are the apps on the go?

Going further, you must inquire about yourself and distinguish between "investing and trading" and which interests you. Investing involves taking a sum of money and dumping it somewhere, hoping it will be fertile and grow into long-term assets. Investing is what you do to save for the luxury of the future from right now instead of low-interest rates from mere bank savings accounts. Meanwhile, trading is the buying and selling of assets within a time frame. Trading is short-term and riskier than investment, which is long-term.

These questions must be examined and answered before investing with an online broker. Trade or invest? Accessible mobile app? What sectors to support or trade-in? While asking these questions is essential, getting practical and efficient answers is difficult. However, there are guides to help with the process.

Choosing the Best Online Broker

The following factors will aid you in the evaluation of a broker.

Commissions

Examine the commission on your most feasible option: there are several options for investment, like bonds, mutual funds, ETFs, etc. Some brokers also offer future trading opportunities.

The investment options the broker offers will set the value for commissions and your subsequent satisfaction. The proposals and their incurred commissions are discussed below:

Individual stocks: while charges are still being attached to the buying and selling of stocks by some brokers, there are a few of them available without commissions; E-Trade, Interactive brokers, etc.

Mutual funds: you can limit mutual funds' transaction costs by purchasing from a company with no-transaction-fee mutual funds. Mutual funds attract an internal fee called "expense ratio," which is charged directly by the funds, not the broker.

ETFs are usually purchased for a price just like shares, making them open to the Broker's stock commission. You could get brokers who offer free commission too.

Account Minimums

While some brokers offer limited accounts, mini- mums, others offer unlimited minimum levels, such as Merrill Edge, Ally Vest, and co.

Account Fees

There is no way to shy away from account fees, but you can minimize them. While some brokers will charge you considerably when transferring to a new broker, the new company sometimes offers reimbursement of your fees through limit bonds.

The annual fees, inactivity fees, trading platform sub, and extra charges are widespread charges, and you can easily boycott any additional charges by not choosing the broker that demands them.

Trade techniques and tech needs

As a beginner investor, you may want a helping hand through your learning and informational videos, tutorials, etc. Depending on the broker, these could be offered free to the investors, but the educational offers are primarily made available to all beginner investors.

Utilize Promotions

Promotions are a better reason to invest in a broker. Still, it could spur a choice between picking one that offers enticing offers to the customer, cash bonuses, and deposit amounts and another that does not.

CHAPTER FOUR

Structures To Manage Your Money

This chapter will look at managing your money, primarily via external structures. We'll discuss Money Managers, Financial Advisors, and Mutual Funds. We'll examine if you need them, and how to decide to choose them. Let's get started, shall we?

As we stated at the beginning of this book, the material in this book was written for people with little to no professional or corporate financial management knowledge who want to invest in the Stock Market, and in the previous chapters, we've examined many of the basics that you will need to know to start to play in the world of stocks and investments. But then, the question arises, should you hire a professional financial adviser to help manage your portfolio and investment?

First, it's important to mention that many people realize they cannot solely depend on a financial advisor to manage their portfolios. The crashing of stocks and other markets in recent years has established the need for anyone investing in any market to research and ensure that they gain knowledge in that area. In other words, whether you hire a financial adviser, you cannot afford to slack off learning about the stock market and researching any stock you buy. After all, it makes no sense to trust someone else with your money when you have no idea what they are planning to do with it.

Choosing or Using a Financial Advisor

A financial advisor is someone that helps you manage your money. They allow you to manage investing, saving, and spending money. A financial advisor usually offers a wide range of services on everything related to money. Now, the level of influence and interaction that the financial advisor has with your funds is up to you and the structure between both parties, that is, you and the advisor. Financial advisor covers many services, including investment planning, financial consulting, and certified financial planners. There are also digital financial management options, such as robot advisors, where you are not necessarily interacting with a human manager. But more on this later.

What can a Financial Advisor do for you?

A financial advisor is an expert in financial matters who provides various services to manage money, investments, and savings. Therein lies the core of financial advising. The influence of technology has made it possible for ordinary people to enter the financial market without formal training. That said, certain kinds of knowledge are available to only those formally trained financially and can access and take advantage of them. In other words, the fact that you can access the stock market in some form and make trades means that you know only some things there is to know about the market. This is where a financial advisor comes in.

A financial advisor can, among many other things, help you assess your financial situation, review your financial goals, and help you chart a path to achieve those goals. So, a financial advisor will examine your assets, expenses, and debts and help you identify how exactly you can improve. They can also help you work to reduce spending, figure out insurance and tax, increase your savings, and invest your money. Since financial advisor has professional expertise and experience, they can significantly help you improve your portfolio. A good financial advisor can be of help when it comes to achieving your goals of financial independence and freedom.

Types of Financial Advisors

There are several types of financial advisors, both in terms of the services offered and the contexts in which the services are provided. Let's look at some of these financial advisors:

CFP: A CFP or Certified Financial Planner helps you do just that, plan your finances. A professional board in your country must issue a license in your country, such as the Certified Financial Planning Board of Standards in the U.S. To become a CFP, people must educate themselves thoroughly, pass a rigorous test, and demonstrate work experience.

These kinds of financial advisors are primarily aimed at helping you create actionable goals for your finances that you should follow to achieve your plan as you go on.

Broker/Stockbroker: This financial advisor assists you with investments and explains how to invest your money. A stockbroker buys or sells financial products (i.e., stocks) for their customers and typically receives a fee for doing this. To become a broker, you must be licensed by the U.S. Security and Exchanges Commission in the US or any other equivalent board in any country where you may be based.

A Registered Investment Advisor: This advisor gives investors advice and recommendations. RIAs are usually registered with the Security and Exchange Commission or some other form of investor, depending on the company's size or size. Some Investment advisors focus on investment portfolios, while others take a more general and holistic view.

Also, it is not uncommon for a particular individual or company to offer the services of more than just one specific discipline. The reason for this is that it is not. It is very realistic for an average person to employ a CFP only to plan their finances and simultaneously hire another broker to solely manage financial instruments and other investments. Many individual economic advisors are licensed to act in multiple offices, or the company they work for offers these services as part of a particular package.

How much does it cost to hire a Financial Advisor?

Perhaps you are already thinking, if a financial advisor is this good, or can offer this level of services, then I should patronize them; well, pump your brakes first. It would help to consider the cost implications of hiring a financial advisor. Many advisors charge different fees at different rates, but here are some more common ones.

Hourly Rates: Some advisors charge between $75 and $350 per hour. The average rates tend to hover around $150.

Set Fees: Some Financial advisors also request a fixed fee for performing a specific work. It could range from a couple hundred to even thousand dollars.

Monthly Fees: This option is usually reserved for those planning to use the advisor or their company's services for a long time. The advisor and the client can work out a specific fee that someone will pay monthly if you utilize their services. The price could also be a portion of the money you sought to invest.

Manage an Ongoing Fee: This scenario is closely related to paying a monthly fee for an ongoing service. These are some of the combinations of fees that financial advisors can charge, and as you can see, they are expensive. Imagine that you must pay a monthly service fee or a percentage of your investment money for the rest of your life, which becomes costly. For this reason, many people are skeptical about using a Financial Advisor.

Should You Use a Financial Advisor?

The choice of whether to use a financial advisor, in the form of a broker, a CFP, or an Investment Advisor, is more of a personal one rather than a general one. In other words, you must look at your circumstances and see if it fits your budget, time, and unique investment strategy. One of the things that you need to consider is the kind of investments you are making and how risky they are. Generally, the more risk you are willing to take on, the more you should be ready to use the services of a financial advisor. For example, if you are investing in mutual funds, there is little need for a financial advisor. However, you want to enter the stock market to purchase individual stocks. In that case, the risks you are taking are more significant, and you should employ the services of a professional to assist you in managing the portfolio.

Another point to consider is the size of your portfolio. The larger your portfolio is, the more likely you will need professional advice. Plus, a broader portfolio account can easily absorb the fees of hiring a financial advisor.

Finally, it would be best if you researched before using a financial advisor. One of the best ways to get a financial advisor is to ask people around you who have enjoyed success in the stock market over a consistent period. While past profits do not guarantee future earnings, it is easier to trust someone with a record of being somewhat successful than someone without much success in the market.

If possible, create a list of as many advisors you'd like to speak to and schedule a conversation with them. It would help if you did that offline, by the way. While online interviews and conversations are good starters, you should not trust a person or company with your hard-earned money without meeting them. When you meet, ask questions about their investment strategy, whose trading style and philosophy they subscribe to, and how they plan to manage your portfolio. Most of the time, the first consultation is free, as it allows you to get to know each other without the pressure of finances forcing you to perform. The other thing is, as this is free, you can meet several and choose one whose mentality suits yours.

When you meet, ensure you do not leave the meeting with doubts about what you're getting into. Do not allow yourself to be deceived with high-sounding and complex language you do not understand. It would help if you insisted that every term you do not understand and every service charge is explained. Of course, you must be fair in your dealings too. Your advisor is a professional and deserves to be paid well for their expertise and sometimes experience.

Digital Alternatives to Financial Advisors

Recently, more brokerage companies have been implementing digital investment management solutions. Two of these new developments are robot- advisors and Online Financial Planning services.

A robot advisor is a digital service that offers simplified and low-cost investment management. To make use of it, you answer a few questions on the brokerage company's website, and then complex algorithms help you build an investment portfolio according to the goals you have set and the risk appetite you have indicated that you are comfortable with. In this way, robot advisors help monitor and balance your investment, ensuring your portfolio is managed correctly. What's more, a robot advisor costs a fraction of what a real-life human financial advisor will cost.

Another option is online financial planning services. This is more like a traditional advisor than a robot advisor. The online service gives you access to human financial advisors who can help you manage your investments, among other things. Some packages grant access to the type of automated investments you'll get from a robot advisor and the ability to consult with a team of financial advice-. Some more expensive alternatives grant you access to the one-on-one service you will receive from a traditional offline advisor.

Surprisingly, both options are relatively cheap, as well as being flexible. Some companies even charge a large percentage of their fees from the profits they help you make. Before you select a financial advisor, primarily online, ensure that you understand everything they offer and possibly speak to their support teams to understand what exactly you will be charged.

Mutual Funds

A mutual fund is a financial vehicle that is made of a pool of money that has been collected from many investors. These funds are then used to invest in assets and securities such as bonds, stocks, instruments in the money market, and other types of investments. A professional money manager manages the portfolio of a mutual fund. They collate the funds' assets and invest them in a diversified portfolio to produce gains for the investors. The objective of a mutual fund is to generate income for the investors. The mutual fund's prospectus states that the portfolio is structured and maintained to match the investment goals.

Investing in a mutual fund gives individual investors such as yourself access to a professionally managed and diversified portfolio of bonds, equities, stocks, and other securities. Every shareholder will gain and lose proportionally to the gains and losses the funds make. Mutual funds tend to invest in many shields, and the fund's overall performance is tracked as a change in the fund's market capitalization, which is an aggregated performance of the individual investments in the portfolio.

Understanding Mutual Funds in Depth

A mutual fund works by aggregating money from multiple investors to build an extensive portfolio, then investing that money in various types of assets. These include bonds, securities, and equities. Thus, the overall value of the mutual fund depends on how each security or investment is performed. So, in purchasing a mutual fund unit, you are buying into the mutual fund's performance or, better still, a part of the portfolio's value. You have invested your money into buying a fraction of many types of assets - a condition that you could not. Have carried were you to support on your own. This makes a mutual fund different from other types of stock investments. A share in a mutual fund represents a share in many different stocks and other assets.

For this reason, the price of a share of a mutual fund is called the Net Asset Value (NAV) per share, sometimes referred to as the NAPS. A mutual fund's NAV is found by dividing the total value of all the securities it holds by the total number of outstanding shares. Outstanding shares are held by all institutional investors, shareholders, insiders, and company officers. Also, the value of a mutual fund's claim can be bought or redeemed at the current NAV, which remains stable, unlike the stock price. The NAV of a mutual fund does not fluctuate but is settled at the end of each trading day.

Income is earned from a mutual fund in 3 significant ways. Interest is made on the dividends in stocks and interest on bonds held in the portfolio of the funds. Generally, a fund pays out most of the funds it receives in a Single year to investors through a distribution. Usually, there is an option for investors to either receive a check or reinvest the earnings to get more shares.

If the fund sells assets that have been appreciated, then the fund is said to have a capital gain. Most funds also transfer these gains to the investors during a distribution at the end of a financial year.

If the fund holdings appreciate but are not sold by the fund manager, the fund shares increase in price, and then you can sell your mutual fund shares on the open market.

Should you invest in a mutual fund?

Why should you consider investing in a mutual fund? For starters, mutual funds help eliminate or at least reduce risk. As we have said in a previous chapter, diversification is essential to keep your chances low. Or put in simple language, you shouldn't put all your eggs in one basket. Consider an investor that invests in Apple or Amazon stocks. The investor would lose money if the buy came before the company had a lousy quarter because all his investment is tied to that company.

On the other hand, somebody will mitigate if the investor uses that money to buy shares in a mutual fund. That is because the mutual fund has stocks in other companies; the loss will count for a small part of the fund's portfolio. In this way, a mutual fund helps you avoid any significant losses, but at the same time, you don't get any big wins either.

Imagine the flip side of our analogy, where Amazon or Apple had a great quarter and outperformed the competition. Any investor investing solely in that company would have made much money. On the other hand, an investor in a mutual fund with a stake in a company will not make as much profit because that company's stocks are only a part of the fund's portfolio. It's a classic risk and reward scenario: the higher your risk, the higher your chances of reward, and vice versa.

It is essential to say that if you are already investing in a retirement package, you are most likely investing in some mutual fund. In this case, you can decide to go for a riskier alternative. You might decide to invest directly in the stocks of a company.

So, as a recap, let us re-examine what we've looked at in this chapter. While you can invest in the stock market on your own, sometimes, it may make sense to look at hiring the services of a professional financial advisor. However, the fees charged by many traditional professional advisors are high and can hurt your portfolio, especially if it isn't ample. A good alternative is a robot advisor or an online financial planning system. These digital platforms provide financial services like traditional financial advisors but usually at a much cheaper rate. They consider your present financial situation and goals and help you plan how to achieve them. Lastly, you can invest in a mutual fund if you are seeking a way to diversify your investment and reduce risk. However, you should know that your profit might tend to be on the low end. Remember, again, high risk, high reward, and low risk, low reward.

Chapter Five

How The Best Of All Time Invest (And What History Shows Us)

They say if you want to be successful at anything, learn from those who are already successful. Thus, in this chapter, we'll look at some of the greatest investors and how they invested. We'll look at trading strategies and how to select the one that is best for you.

But first, what is an investment strategy, and what types do we have?

What is an Investment Strategy?

If your plan to invest in the long term can be likened to a football match, your investment portfolio is your game plan. The right investment strategy can and will increase your chances of success. To achieve financial freedom, you need to have a solid plan for managing your investments. I advise that you have an investment strategy before placing your first trade. It's the second thing you need to learn how to do immediately after you know what a stock quote is and how to buy it.

Why is it Important to Define Your Strategy?

The right investment strategy is like having an instruction manual to guide you through the investment process. It will help you identify and pick the suitable investments for you and your goals and avoid investments that look promising but will perform poorly over time.

When creating an investment strategy, you must precisely determine your goals. A proper investment strategy starts with a concrete plan you are trying to achieve. For example, a goal like "to be financially independent" or 'to be able to retire early,' while being a good and noble goal, is unrealistic and cannot help you make concrete and realistic progress. Instead, you should set a goal: "I want to achieve an annual return rate of 7% on my investment contributions over the next 15 years, to amass $600,000, that I can retire on." The more specific your goals are, the easier it is to decide how exactly to make progress toward achieving the goals. This is doubly important if you are not hiring an investment manager. This means that you must be meticulous about investing your money. There are many investment strategies; the real work is finding the one that fits your goals and circumstances. The golden key to success is to pair the right plan with the right goals.

In addition to the right goals, you need to represent your current financial situation accurately. How much does it cost you to live? What are your monthly expenses? How much debt are you in? Can you handle debt? What are your spending habits, and how often do you save? Often, investment fails in the long term because of consistency and good management. It would help to consider the impact that investment will have on your finances so that you don't get into trouble halfway. If you can afford it, you can speak to a CFP to help create a plan. While you do not need to have them on retainer, their expertise can help you when you start investing.

The next thing you need to decide is what your risk tolerance is. I've spoken extensively throughout this book about risk and risk tolerance. Risk tolerance talks about how much risk you will expose your investment to. For example, putting all your assets on a single stock is quite risky because a fall in the price of that stock will mean that all your investment loses value, and a rise will mean that all your investments will increase in value. Some factors should consider your risk tolerance, such as age, income, and how long you have until you retire. Generally, the younger you are, the more risk you can take because you have more time to recoup any losses.

Let's look at some of the greatest investors and their investment strategies.

Benjamin Graham's Investment Philosophy

When it comes to investment philosophies, one person that is worth looking at is Benjamin Graham. He is known as the father of value investing, an investment style many modern-day investors adopt. But first, let's look at who Benjamin Graham was and how he got to Wall Street.

Early Years

Benjamin Graham was born in London in 1894 but moved to New York as an infant with his family. Graham was a gifted academician and won a scholarship to Columbia University and eventually graduating second in his class. His family lost their savings in the Bank Panic of 1907. He joined Wall Street due to the financial pressures of his family, as his father had died, and he needed to become the family breadwinner. He turned down a teaching position at Columbia University and took an entry-level job at Newburger, Hender, and Loeb. Graham had risen through the ranks within a few years. He moved from runner to clerk, to market letter writer, to analyst, and finally became a partner at age 26.

He left Newburger in 1923 to start his firm and partnered with Jerry Newman to launch Graham- Newman.

How his Trading Style was built

In the early days of Benjamin Graham, he set the foundation for building a systematic method of fundamental analysis, one of the methods of analyzing a company. During this period, the rest of Wall Street depended on rumors and insider tips to make large profits. However, Graham sought mate information about any company wherever he could before making decisions.

Before the SEC was created in the 1930s, company information was scarce. Only insiders in a company and moguls on Wall Street had access to this information. However, the average investor was left in the dark. With the resources available, Graham could search for and find many pieces of relevant information, thus gaining an edge in the market.

For example, one of Graham's first big waves as an investor was on a popularly called "Northern Pipeline Affair." Northern Pipeline was one of the companies spun off from Standard Oil when they were ordered to break up by the court. As a fellow on Wall Street, he discovered this company was trading at a discount to a portfolio of liquid securities and cash. The shares were trading at

$65 a share, while the cash share and high-grade bonds were worth $90 a share. Graham then took a position and attempted to convince management to distribute the investment portfolio to shareholders. Management and shareholders were, however, not convinced. When He failed to win the board over, he took more decisive action, fighting by proxy for two seats on the board. After winning both seats, the commission agreed to distribute the excess capital.

Value Investing and Books

The crash of the stock market in 1929 caused Graham to lose almost all of the investments that he had made and subsequently taught him critical things about the stock market. His observations throughout the crash and as he rebuilt drove him to publish a book called *Security Analysis* with his former student David Dodd. Another great American investor, Irving Kahn, contributed to the book's content.

The book was published in the early days of the Great Depression in 1934 when Graham lectured at the Columbia Business School. This book taught the basics of the Value Investment strategy. This strategy involves buying stocks that are currently undervalued and have enormous growth potential as time goes on. It is important to note that at this time, people viewed the stock market as a speculative vehicle, and the idea of an intrinsic safety margin or value was first espoused by the book *Security Analysis.* The concept of fundamental analysis is a system where the business or company itself is studied, rather than the market, was espoused by the book.

As taught by Dodd and Graham, the idea behind a value investment strategy is to derive the stock's intrinsic value without considering the current market price. Investors can determine a stock's intrinsic value by considering company factors like earnings, assets, and dividends. If it is determined that the stock's intrinsic value is much higher than the current price, then the buyer should purchase shares in that company and hold them till there is a mean reversion. The mean reversion is an idea that as time passes, the intrinsic and market price will move closer and converge at a price that reflects the stock's actual value. This would occur if the market were efficient, a theory that Graham believed in. If the market is efficient, a company's intrinsic value will eventually be reflected by the change in market price.

Graham also believed in a margin of safety provided for by investors' irrationality, such as their lack of ability to predict the future and market variations. This, Graham argues, is certain to deliver a safety margin or space for human error that the investor can invest in.

Let's take an example of how this method works. If you were an investor considering purchasing stocks in a company X. The company is well-known and is a leader in its industry. The stores are trading at

$100 per share; meanwhile, it earns $10 per year as a profit. Meanwhile, a competing company Y is a younger company that is not as well-known but earns less, at $2 per year. The stock is also valued at $15 per year, which is much cheaper.

Using Benjamin Graham's method of investing, somebody will use these, and other figures will be used to perform a fundamental analysis of the company. In this case, company Y is cheaper than company X to buy every dollar of earnings. The Price to earnings ratio (we covered this in Chapter 2) for company X is 10, while for company Y is 7.5. Using Benjamin Graham's method of investing, you will conclude that the stocks of Company X are over-priced because of their popularity. As such, the investor will be better served to choose to invest in buying the stocks in Company Y.

In 1949, Graham wrote the widely acclaimed book. *The Intelligent Investor: The Definitive Book on Value Investing.* This book is widely considered the bible of value investing and features a character known as Mr. Market, a metaphor for market price mechanics. Mr. Market is the imaginary business partner who tries to sell shares to or buy shares from the investor. Mr. Market is ofttimes irrational and shows up at the investor's doorstep with varying prices depending on how optimistic or pessimistic he feels today. This is an analogy of the irrationality of the market. Of course, the investor is not obligated to accept any offer at any time. Graham's point is that instead of relying on daily market sentiments, which.

If run on the greed and fear of investors, an investor should analyze how much a company's stock is worth based on the company's reports of its operations and financial position. According to Graham, the intelligent investor sells to optimists and buys from pessimists.

In another chapter, we cover value investing in more detail, but I want you to be familiar with this philosophy. Successful investors, such as Warren Buffet, a literal student of Graham in his classes at Columbia University and a student of Graham's investing methods, adopted this same philosophy. **Warren Buffet's Investment Philosophy**

Warren Buffet is the most well-known investor of the 20th and 21st centuries. He has consistently maintained a high ranking on Forbes' list of billionaires. His investment strategy has reached mythical heights; many other brokers and investors claim to follow it. Warren Buffet follows some necessary tents and an investment philosophy that is now extremely popular and widely followed around the globe.

Brief Background

Buffet formed the Buffet Partnership Ltd. In 1956, less than ten years later, by 1965, it was in control of Berkshire Hathaway. By June 2006, he announced his plans to donate his entire fortune to charity.

Investment Philosophy

Warren Buffet's investment philosophy is heavily influenced by the thoughts espoused by Benjamin Graham, with Buffet credited with saying, "I'm 85% Benjamin Graham". Like Benjamin, Buffet's investing style involves finding undervalued and average companies and diversifying his investment portfolio through them. His investment philosophy might look, but it is complex.

First, Warren Buffet only restricts himself to investing in businesses he understands and can analyze successfully. He considers an in-depth understanding of how a company operates to be a viable forecast of how the business will perform.

As we said, value investing involves looking for and finding currently underpriced stocks. As such, they expect their values to rise as the intrinsic value and market price converge. Buffet, however, takes this to another level. He isn't concerned with the supply and demand intricacies of the stock market. He isn't worried about the stock market's activities at all. His famous quote demonstrates this mentality: "In the short term, the market is a popularity contest, and in the long term, it is a weighing machine."

Therefore, his philosophy is to choose stocks based on the company's overall potential. Selecting and holding stocks is a long-term play. The Buffet isn't seeking capital gain in this investment philosophy, but ownership in quality companies can generate earnings. Thus, when Buffet invests in a company, he isn't so much bothered about whether the market will recognize its worth; instead, he's more concerned about how well that company can make money as a business, which makes all the difference.

Warren Buffet's Methodology

To select companies that are valuable but under- priced, he asks some crucial questions about himself and the company. A direct relationship exists between the stock price and its level of excellence. Warren Buffet understands this, and he carefully examines this relationship. Of course, apart from this, different factors need to be analyzed too. This relationship is merely one of the criteria you must remember while selecting stocks or a company to invest in.

Company's Performance: The return on equity or ROE often measures a company's performance. It is also known as the stockholder's return on investment. It primarily showcases the rate at which the investors earn income on their shares. By comparing one company's ROE with other companies, Warren Buffet usually determines how well a company performs within a given Industry. The net income divided by shareholder's equity provides the return on equity. Before deciding to analyze the company's performance history, Buffet will carefully go through the ROE of a given company for the previous 5-10 years.

Level of Debt: Another ratio commonly used to measure whether a company's value will increase in the future is the debt-to-equity ratio. The portion of the debt is always supposed to be relatively lower than the equity present in the company. Only when the level of debt is trimmed will the earnings generated from the shareholder's equity increase. A higher level of debt shows that the company needs to perform better. Divide a company's total liabilities by the shareholder's equity to calculate the debt-to-equity ratio. This ratio gives a bird's eye view of the proportion of funds used by a company for financing its assets. If this ratio is high, then it means that the company is relying on debt to finance its purchases. A high debt-to-equity ratio generates earnings volatility and higher expenses incurred toward interest payments.

Profit Margin: You can calculate the company's margin by dividing the net income by the net sales. The simplest way to determine a company's profitability is by looking at its profit margin. A reasonable profit margin combined with the scope for increasing the profit margin shows that the company is highly profitable. Usually, a seasoned investor like Warren Buffet will check the profit margins for the previous 5 or 10 years. A high-profit margin and an increase in this margin show that the company is adept at managing its finances and optimally utilizing its funds.

Company Status: Buffet usually opts for companies that have been around for at least ten years. This criterion effectively eliminates all those companies which have had their IPO (Initial Public Offering) within the last decade. He created this system because it helps him invest only in companies he thoroughly understands. He seldom invests in the newer tech companies coming up these days. Value investing is based on investing in undervalued companies that have been around for a while so that their track record can be carefully analyzed. It is one factor you must consider, and don't solely rely on a company's track record while investing.

Reliance of Commodities: Warren Buffet only invests in a business whose products are unique from its competitors. Apart from this, he also avoids investing in companies that don't offer anything special. If the product offered by a company is not unique, it means that others can easily replace it. Only when a need has a competitive advantage will it be able to increase its value in the future. Or it has to offer something the competitors need help duplicating quickly.

Costs Involved: This brings us to Buffet's final factor while finalizing an investment. Finding a company meeting all the criteria mentioned above might be relatively easy. However, it might be challenging to find one which not only satisfies all the conditions discussed up until now while still being undervalued. Determining the company's intrinsic value and analyzing the business fundamentals are quintessential at this stage. This is trickier than merely calculating the liquidation value if somebody sold the company today. However, it excludes certain intangibles, such as the brand name and identity. Once the company's intrinsic value has been determined, it is compared to the current market capitalization, which is the current total worth of the company. If the inherent value measured is 25% higher than the market cap, then the company is viewed as valuable and can be invested in.

As simple as this sounds, the entire process depends on how accurately you can judge the company.

Peter Lynch's Investment Philosophy

Another of the most successful and well-known investors of all time, he came into the limelight in the late '90s and early 2000s. He was appointed a portfolio manager of the Fidelity Magellan mutual fund in May 1977. Incidentally, this was his first job as a portfolio manager, and he succeeded in growing the asset fund from $20 million to the biggest mutual fund in the world. Moreover, he consistently outperformed the market by a whopping 13.4% annually. The most significant part of all this is that Peter Lynch achieved this by using basic principles that he is happy to share with anyone that cares to listen to. Lynch firmly believes that individual investors have an inherent advantage over larger firms because they can't or won't invest in smaller-cap companies that haven't received considerable attention from analysts and mutual funds. He detailed his strategy in his best-selling book "One Up on Wall Street," written in 1989, and another in 1994 named "*Beating the Street.*"

Peter Lynch's investment is somewhat like that of Warren Buffet and can be summed into 3 points,

Only Buy What You Understand: According to Lynch, our eyes, ears, and common sense are the most excellent stock market research tools we possess. Lynch was proud that his most significant stock market ideas were discovered while strolling in the grocery store or casually chatting with family and friends. He believes we can all perform first-hand analysis as we take in information from the world around us; it merely depends on how we process it. While traveling, driving, reading the dailies, or any other mundane tasks, you can as well discover new investment opportunities. If consumers represent two-thirds of the United States GDP, it means that most of the businesses on the stock market are in business to serve an individual customer. Thus, if something about a company attracts you as a consumer, you should consider paying more attention to it to invest. **Do Your Research Thoroughly:** Picking a company you are attracted to, and love is one thing, but you must do a thorough and comprehensive research before investing. Do not confuse the seeming simplicity of the philosophy to mean that research does not play a significant role in the success Lynch recorded. Lynch highlights some fundamental values when selecting stocks you want to invest in.

Percentage of Sales: If a product or service attracted you to a company, then you should check what percentage of sales that product makes to be meaningful. A great product or service that doesn't make more than 5 to 10% of the company's total sales will have minimal, if any, impact on the company's bottom line.

PEG Ratio: Peter Lynch is credited with inventing the Price-to-Earnings Growth ratio. It is the valuation ratio to the rate at which the company's earnings are growing. This ratio tells you how much expectation is built into the stock, and as such, you want to invest in companies with a healthy growth rate of earnings and reasonable valuations. A company with a steady growth rate with a PEG ratio of two or more already has the earnings growth built into the stock price already, leaving little to no room for error.

Select Companies that have strong cash positions and debt-to-equity ratios that are below average. Companies with stable cash flows and assets that are prudently managed to give the company options in all market environments.

Invest for the long term: Lynch firmly believes in investing in the long-term game. He said that "absent of many surprises, stocks have been relatively predictably stable for the last 10 – 20 years. You might as well flip a coin to decide whether they'll be higher in the next two or three years". While this kind of speech from someone on Wall Street might seem surprising, it shows how much he believed in his philosophy. Lynch conducted a study with unexpected results. The study was to determine whether timing the market was an effective strategy to jump on.

According to the strategy's results, if an investor had invested $1,000 per year on the day stocks were at their absolute high for that year for 30 years, ranging from 1965 – 1995, that investor would have earned a compounded return of 10,6%. Meanwhile, if another investor invests $1,000 every year for the same 30 years on the day the stocks were at their lowest for the year, this investor will have earned 11.7% compound interest. In other words, after 30 years of investing at the worst possible time, the first investor trailed the second by a mere 1.1% per year. This is why Lynch believes that trying to predict the direction the market will move quickly is not worth the effort. Somebody will better spend that time researching a picking a strong company. If the company is strong, the stocks will appreciate as the business makes more money.

In conclusion, there is a seeming emphasis on picking and investing in the best and healthiest companies; better put, the greats favor a strategy about precision. In other words, you must work to do the research and find out how dependable and profitable the company is likely to be in the future.

Chapter Six

Active Investing Strategies

Now we have examined how to choose an investment strategy, as well. We will discuss some of the investment strategies famous and successful investors have used in this chapter and the following active and passive investment strategies.

What are Active Investment Strategies?

Active investment strategies are just that, strategies that require your active participation. It would help if you did loads of research, pay attention to the company's financials, etc. It is quite tasking, to be honest, but the rewards are lucrative. If you select a good enough company, you can hit it big. For example, if you invested in Netflix. As far back as 2003, when a share was spilled adjusted for less than $5, your stake will have risen to $40 in 2004, a meteoric rise of 700% in less than a year. Of course, you might not always make the right call, but with stocks like this, you might only need one to recoup all your losses. Before discussing this further, let's look at Fundamental analysis and why it is crucial for active investing strategies.

Fundamental Analysis

Fundamental analysis is one of the ways of viewing the business at a basic financial level. This sort of analysis looks at the critical ratios of the company to decipher how healthy the business is, financially speaking. Fundamental research also shows you what common stock's value should be like. Several components are considered: revenue, earnings, the business's cost, interest rates, and asset management.

Many speculators utilize Fundamental Analysis in isolation, but it may be helpful to combine it with other tools to value the stocks before deciding to invest—the objective of using Fundamental. The analysis is to figure out the stock's present worth and, more importantly, how to stock is valued by the market.

Should you not be planning to do the fundamental analysis by yourself, understanding the terms and key ratios used to evaluate a company will allow you to follow a company's stock carefully and decipher which will be the best to invest in.

It's About the Earnings

Fundamental analysis and investment portfolios are all about profit. Investors want to be aware of the profit the company is making right now and the future profit potential. It might be complex to calculate; however, the most important thing about choosing a stock to invest in and determining a rising stock price often indicates a regular dividend. If the earnings do not meet the projected cost, it can bring down the price of the shares. Businesses report the profits made each quarter. As such, analysts use these reports to examine the company's health and then raise the alarm when the companies do not make expected earnings.

Tools used for fundamental analysis.

As significant as earnings may be, they usually only show you something meaningful with another input source. Revenues alone do not entirely capture how the market values a stock. You will need additional fundamental analysis tools to construct a perfect image of how the market loves the store.

Some Ratios that You Need to Know

While we've covered most of the ratios you should know in Chapter 3, we'll review a few important ones again for fundamental analysis.

Most of these ratios are not that hard to find out, and what's more, you can see most of these ratios already calculated on many financial websites like MSN MoneyCentral or CNN Money. In any case, if you ever need to calculate them yourself, you should note that the essential tools for Fundamental Analysis depend on growth, market value, and profit. Here are the ratios that are important for you to learn:

Earnings Per Share (EPS): Each stock reflects the amount of the company's profit. EPS calculated as the net income on the selected shares is then divided by the available shares.

Price to Earnings Ratio (P/E): The P/E ratio compares the stock's selling price to the company's earnings per share.

Projected Earnings Growth (PEG): This ratio anticipates the rate at which the stock earnings grow.

Price to Sales Ratio (P/S): The P/S ratio shows the value of a company's stock compared to the revenue. It is also known as Revenue, sales multiple, or PSR.

The dividend payout ratio is obtained by comparing the dividends paid to Stockholders to the company's net income. It is what accounts for payment that doesn't get paid out externally but is retained to be used for growth that is potentially possible.

Price-to-Book Ratio: This ratio is also called the price-to-equity ratio. It compares the market price of a stock to its book value. To get this, we divide the most recent closing price of the stock by the book value of each share of the last quarter; the asset's value as it is found in the books of the company is the book value. It is the asset's cost minus the cumulative depreciation.

Dividend yield: the ratio of the share price compared to the yearly dividend. It is written in percentage form. To get this, divide the dividends paid within a year by the share's value.

Return on equity (ROE): we get this by dividing the net income by shareholders' equity. This gives us a return on equity (ROE). It can also be called the firm's return on net worth.

Remember that all the above numbers are tools, so you should not use any single number or ratio in insulation. They can't give you a suggestion to buy or sell by themselves; instead, we should use them in conjunction with other ratios. Well, you are looking for the perfect stock to invest in; all these ratios should be the benchmark used to gauge the value of that potential investment.

Value Investing

The first type of active investing strategy that we will look at is value investing. Value investors are more or fewer shoppers looking for a bargain. They seek out undervalued stocks, then buy them and expect their values to increase as time goes on. In value investing, the Investor is looking for stocks that they believe have lower prices than the intrinsic value of such security. Value investing is based on some level of irrationality in the market. It is this irrationality that value investors, in theory, seek to profit from. It presents an opportunity to buy a stock at a discounted price and wait for the value to increase.

A value investor can find a deal without combing through volumes of financial data to find a bargain. Many Mutual funds allow investors to select and invest in undervalued stocks. For instance, the Russell 1000 value index is a famous benchmark value investors use, and many mutual funds imitate this index.

The underlying mentality behind Value Investing is that you are not just buying a stock but a company. Thus, a value investor looks at more than store performance charts. Instead, more attention is paid to the company. In other words, the value investor examines the company it believes will increase in value the most over time and then invests in it.

However, value investing can be tricky because valuing a business is usually subjective. Everyone has access to the same information. The valuation that is made based on this information can vary quite widely. This is because different investors do have varying levels of risk tolerance. The company's intrinsic value is almost entirely subjective and depends on the investor's industry knowledge and personal bias. So, while you can look at the historical data, it does not necessarily guarantee a trend in the future. The real trick of value investing is to buy something that you know is currently worth less than it is, why you do not see how much it will be worth. You should remember that value investing is not just about buying undervalued stocks but buying good stocks currently undervalued. For this reason, successful value investors advise beginners to invest in Industries they are conversant with and confident in. The more you know about an industry, the more accurate your judgment about a company and its stock in that industry is likely to be.

How to Pick Profitable Stocks

Let's look at how to select good stocks to invest in. When picking stocks to invest in, you should focus more on the company than the price stocks themselves. By this, I mean that you should see yourself as a stakeholder and the company owner because that is what you are. When you buy a stock in a company that is publicly traded, purchasing a portion of the company's ownership. So, as a value investor, you should view yourself as though you were the company's sole owner. If you were to be the company's sole owner, how diligent would you be with your research? That is the attitude you want to use when doing the fundamental analysis of any company you are interested in before you decide to invest in their stocks. It would help if you remembered that bang and trading stocks are a long-term goal rather than a short-term one, usually looking at a minimum of 5 to 10 years of holding the stock. This is why you should do extensive before investing in a particular company.

When researching stocks, keep your eyes open for those that have:

High Dividend Yield: This is the percentage paid to the investors from the store compared to its price, the higher this value is, the more valuable the stock is. However, it would help if you only came here with results in the same industry to get an accurate result.

Low Price to Book Ratio: As I explained, this ratio compares the book value and market value is the better the company is. This hints at what will be left if the company gets liquidated.

A Low Price to Earnings Ratio: compare the share's price to what it will earn. The goal is to pay less for the stock and profit more.

Any real value investing is in the investing game for the long term. You must be able to look past temporary losses and see the big picture. A perfect example of this is seen in Warren Buffet. When investing in value, he does his homework on companies, sometimes analyzing them for years before purchasing a stock, but once he does, he is committed to the long-term. For example, when Warren Buffett invested quite heavily in the airline industry, she was quoted as saying that the airlines "had a bad first century" and that he hoped that they had gotten that century out of the way. The choice of the stocks to invest in properties should be based on decades of evidence of that company's performance and is also made with a decade of future performance in mind.

Value Investing Tools

Traditionally, value investing requires the Investor to perform detailed and exhaustive research. However, beginner investors may need more time or skill for that research detail. The P/E ratio has rapidly been adopted as the primary tool investors use to identify cheap or undervalued stocks quickly. As we said earlier, this number comes by dividing the share price of a stock by the earnings-per-share of the same stock. A lower P/E ratio usually means paying less than $1 of the current earnings. Therefore, value investors typically look for companies that have lesser Price-Earnings ratios.

While the Price-Earnings ratio is quite a good place to start, many experts insist that more is needed to make the strategy function as effectively as it should. The Financial Analysts Journal published the research which stated that: "strategies that involved quantitative investment based on this kind of ratio were not a good enough substitute for the strategy of value investing that make use of a more comprehensive approach to locate and identify stocks that are undervalued," According to the research, the reason many investors are usually confused and lured in by the low PE ratio stocks that are based on accounting numbers that are generally temporarily imported. Many times, caused by false high-earning figures, which is the denominator in the equation used to calculate the PE ratio. When the actual earnings are reported eventually, they are usually lower than analysts forecasted. Thus, a return to the true mean ensues. In other words, the P/E ratio increases, and the intrinsic value the investor thought to invest in suddenly vanishes.

To avoid becoming victims, the researchers advised investors to utilize quantitative approaches to detect such anomalies, such as combining values derived from the PE formula with momentum profitability and quality measures to avoid the so-called value traps.

In conclusion, value investing will work only when those investing are prepared to stick with such a company for an extended period and is also ready to put in serious efforts to research the stock. A study by Dodge and Cox showed that value investing strategies almost always perform better than growth.

They were investing in strategies when viewed over ten years or even more. The result of the research then showed that value investing strategies only performed worse than growth investing strategies for three 10-year periods when we view the previous 90 years as a case study. These periods were the Great Depression. Which spanned from 1929 to 1940, the bubble of the technology stock, which took place between 1989 – 1999 and the years between 2004 and 2014/15

Growth Investing

This is the second type of active investing strategy. In this strategy, they are looking for undervalued stocks, and group investors lookout for investments with the potential for solid growth in the future. An investor employing a growth investing strategy is looking for a company that will produce the following significant phenomena. However, good investing is not just some reckless method of speculative investing; instead, it is the ability to evaluate the current health of the stock and its growth potential. Successful growth investing must consider the prospect available to the company as a result of the sector that it is in. For example, you will have to think if electric vehicles have a future. Before you decide to invest in a company like Tesla, consider if artificial intelligence will soon become Commonplace before you choose to invest in a data science company. For this service or product offered by a company to grow, there needs to be evidence that somebody will widely accept such a product or service and that there is a robust appetite in the market for such a product. Growth investors answer these questions by examining the company's recent history. This is done because, in theory, a growth company's stock should be growing; that is, the organization should be able to show a trend of earnings that is strong and consistent, proving the company's ability to meet investors' growth expectations.

One of the disadvantages of group investing, however, is that there are few to no dividends. Growing companies usually need capital to maintain their expansion, meaning there will be little cash left to pay investors dividends. Moreover, growth with faster endings also comes with higher valuations, creating a much higher risk for many investors.

Is growth investing effective?

Research shows that a value investing strategy tends to perform better than a growth investing strategy when viewed in the long term; this does not mean that growth investors do not profit from their plans. A study by the Stern Business School at New York University reported, "While growth investing underperforms value investing for long periods, there existed shorter sub-periods in which a growth investing strategy did dominate. The major challenge of growth investing is determining where such "sub-periods" will happen.

It is interesting to note that we can determine when a group strategy will likely perform better than a value investing strategy by looking at the National Gross Domestic Product, or GDP. This is seen if you look at the years 2000 - 2015 throughout this period, including strategy value strategy for seven out of the fifteen years (2007, 2008, 2009, 2011, 2013, 2014, and 2015)). The GDP growth rate was less than 2% for five of those seven years. On the other hand, a strategy based on value investing outperformed a growth strategy for nine years and seven out of these. In nine years, the Gross Domestic Product was higher than 2%. We can see that the growth investing strategy tends to be more profitable when the GDP is reduced.

Growth Vs. Value Investing

Which strategy do you use? Do you concentrate on growth or value? Which of these strategies will generate a better ROI in the long run? Historically, growth stocks tend to do better when the interest rates and GDP decrease while a company's earnings increase. On the other hand, value stocks do well when the economy is recovering but do not do so well when the market is going through a bullish phase.

All those interested in investing in the long run usually invest in a combination of value and growth stocks to mitigate the risks involved while increasing the chances of earning higher rates of return. This approach will allow an investor to earn profits in a usual market condition where somebody will recover somebody any losses made, and the returns will increase over time.

Chapter Seven

Passive Investing

So far, we have examined active investing strategies where you must do a book of research and follow up on the stocks you've purchased to ensure that you make your desired profit. However, passive investing is a good alternative for those who need more time, patience, or the required skill to do this research. Passive investing is an investment strategy that seeks to maximize the Returns investigated by minimizing buying and selling. One common passive investing strategy is index investing, where an investor purchases benchmark representation such as the S&P 500 index and holds it for a relatively long time.

Passive Investing

Passive investing generally refers to a buy-and-hold portfolio strategy aimed at a long-term investment horizon and, thus, has a minimal trading horizon in the market.

Passive investment is generally cheaper, less complex, and often produces superior results after tax when considered for medium and long-time horizons compared to actively managed portfolios.

Index Investing

This is a passive investment strategy; whose goal is to generate returns like that of a broad market index. Investors use index investing to reproduce the performance of a specific index, such as fixed income or detailed index, by buying exchange-traded funds (ETFs) that are built to track the underlying index closely. Index investing has several advantages. Research has shown that index investing tends to perform beyond and above active portfolio management when viewed over a longer time frame. Also, the hands-off approach that passive investing utilizes helps eliminate many of the biases and uncertainties that arise with an actively managed portfolio.

Understanding Passive Investing

Passive investing methods avoid the limited performances and fees of frequently making trades (buying and selling stocks). The goal of a passive investor is to build wealth gradually. Thus, passive investing is also known as a buy-and-hold strategy; they buy security and consider owning it long-term. Unlike the case of active investing, a passive investor does not seek to profit from short-term price fluctuations or changes in the market timing. The idea behind passive investing is that the market will post positive returns over a long period.

A passive investment manager will generally make you believe that it is challenging to out-think the market and requires more considerable effort; as such, they seek to match sector or market performance. Passive investment attempts to replicate the performance of the market by building a well-diversified portfolio of single stocks that will have otherwise required extensive research if done individually. Index funds were introduced in the 1970s and easily achieved returns aligned with the market. When exchange-traded funds or ETFs, which track major indices such as the SPDR S&P 500 ETF (SPY), came in the 1990s, the process was simplified further by allowing investors to trade index funds themselves as though they were stocks.

Pros and Cons of Passive Investing

A well-diversified portfolio is essential to investing successfully, and passive investing is an excellent way to achieve this diversification. Index funds, used in passive investing, spread risk by holding all or a representative sample of the securities in their target benchmarks. The goal of an index fund is to track a target benchmark or index rather than seeking stocks that are winners of buyers; hence, they avoid constantly selling or buying Securities. This helps eliminate transaction fees and operating expenses from an actively managed investment portfolio. An index fund offers investors simplicity and an easy way to invest in any closing market because it tracks an index. There is little or no need to monitor an individual manager or choose among several investment teams.

On the other hand, however, passive investing is subject to total market risk because of index funds. Track the entire market. When there's an overall fall in the stock market, or the prices of bonds fall, index funds also follow suit. Managers of index funds are generally prohibited from taking defensive measures such as reducing a position in shares, even when it looks obvious and the manager thinks that the prices of shares will fall. Index funds that are passively managed first constraints on their performance as they are naturally designed to track the benchmark index rather than attempt to perform exceptionally well.

Some of the pros of passive investing are:

- **Meager fees:** Because there is nobody selecting stocks. Oversight is much less expensive. Passive funds follow the index that they used as the benchmark.

- **Tax efficiency:** passive investing is typically tax-efficient because the strategy does not result in a substantial capital gains tax for that financial year

- **Transparency:** what assets are in an index fund?

- **Simplicity:** a group of policies or an individual index is much easier to comprehend, manage, and implement than a complex and dynamic strategy that requires consistent research and management.

A potential drawback of passive investing is that the potential returns are more diminutive. By the very definition of passive investment, even during times of market upheaval. Passive Investments might occasionally beat the market; they will rarely post the significant returns active managers seek unless there is a boom in the market itself. Active managers can, on the other hand, bring in more substantial rewards while, of course, taking on more risk. Will an extension of the same old rule, the higher the risk, the more the premium, and vice versa?

Why are Index Funds Popular?

One of the main reasons index funds are quite popular among investors is because of the immediate diversification they offer. As mentioned in the earlier chapters, diversifying investment portfolios helps mitigate the risk of loss. With a single purchase of index funds, an investor can effectively invest in stocks of different companies. For instance, whenever an investor invests in an index fund based on the S&P 500 index, the investor can access the ownership of stocks in 500 companies. This is an excellent strategy to reduce the risk of investments from a loss you might have gained had you invested in just one company. Funds like the S&P 500 index funds allow you to invest in different companies across various industries. However, certain index funds will enable you to invest only in certain sectors, countries, or even specific types of investments. This is one of the reasons why the S&P 500 index funds are amongst the most popular index fund options. Apart from diversity, their return is high, and the risks involved in trading are low. As with other stocks, fluctuations can creep in, but historically, index funds provide a consistent return of around 10% in profits annually.

Best Index Funds for 2022

Now that we've talked a bit about passive investing and index funds, it's time to look at some of the best index funds in 2022 as a guide to investing your money and starting your journey to financial freedom.

We'll look at Vanguard as they are one of the best and biggest index funds on the planet. Investing in Vanguard funds is a little complicated compared to using a simple robot Advisor. Before we go further, we must touch a little on fees. Even though I explain this in Chapter 2, you should understand the expenses involved. Don't overlook this aspect because it can cost you 1-25% of your earnings from investing. This is simply atrocious, and it gets many beginner investors to turn to index funds like Vanguard in the first place.

Even if you aren't too keen on passive investing, it is prudent to start using Personal Capital Fee Analyzer to check the fees payable on your investment account.

Also, before I go on, let's quickly establish the difference between an ETF and a mutual fund. Vanguard defined ETF as a collection of numerous stocks and bonds in a single fund, similar to an index fund. The one significant difference is that you can automate your investments using mutual funds. However, opt for an ETF if you want to reduce the amount payable as fees and aren't averse to manually making your monthly contributions. Vanguard offers mutual funds and ETFs but has different risk-reward ratios and prices. For a Vanguard ETF, you can start with as low as $1. On the other hand, the minimum initial investment can be between $1000 and $3000 while investing with Vanguard Mutual Funds.

Total Stock Market (ETF) - VTI

NYSEARCA: VTI | Vanguard | Morningstar | Fee: 0.04% | 5 Year Avg: 9.58%.

This is the Vanguard flagship fund, and it is still their best. This ETF is a Vanguard Total Stock Market Index Fund share class. It is a blend of large, medium, and small-cap companies in the US and tracks the performance of the CRSP US Total market index.

This fund has the lowest expense ratio I've ever seen because it tracks a few smaller indexes, allowing it to be mostly automated. When most people mention investing in Vanguard, they usually refer to this fund. This fund is so successful that 92% of fund managers cannot beat this.

Social Index fund (Investor Shares)

Mutual Fund from Vanguard with a Fee of 0.18% and a % year average of 10.89%

This VTI has an element of socially responsible investing applied to it. It is aimed at companies that are either environmentally sustainable or focus on the social impact of their operations and activities. These companies use renewable energy to power their activities or support equal pay for all genders. Some companies that follow these strategies are Tesla, Apple, Google, and Microsoft. Reducing the cost of energy or attracting the best of talents are suitable for the business, and as such, it is not all that surprising that this fund performs than VTI.

Vanguard Target Retirement 2050 Fund (Investor Shares) – VFIFX

Mutual Funds from Vanguard with a Fee of 0,15% and a 5-year average of 6.25%. This fund is a life-cycle type of fund. In other words, the risk tolerance and investing direction change as you, the investor, grow in age and your investment goals change. It starts with most of the portfolio invested in stocks, and then assets are gradually relocated.

As time passes, the entire point of the life-cycle fund is to take risks at a younger age and slowly reduce the risk you are under as you get closer to retirement so that market fluctuations and changes do not affect your required money.

While this could be better regarding the fees, it helps bridge a gap in most people's portfolios. The number in the fund name, such as "2050," corresponds to your regular retirement date.

SPDR S&P 500 ETF Trust (SPY)

The SPDR S&P 500 ETF started the wave of ETF investing and has been around since 1993. It is a popular investment option, even today. With over

With $262 billion in assets, it is amongst the most popular and largest ETFs available. The industry titans, State Street Global Advisors, sponsor this fund and track the S&P 500. The expense ratio is 0.09%, meaning every $10,000 invested will cost about $9 annually.

This is amongst the best S & P 500 indices available. This investing option gives investors access to owning S&P 500 stocks at a marginal cost and the benefits of diversification of investment portfolio and risk management. Because of all these benefits, it is certainly not surprising that these are believed to be the most significant funds on the market today. If you want to invest passively, these are your best options.

CHAPTER EIGHT

What Are Diversification and Asset Allocation?

When it comes to protecting your investments, diversification and asset allocation are some tactics you can use, this chapter examines diversification and asset allocation and how to use these to safeguard your Investment Portfolio from losses and increase gains.

What Is Diversification?

Diversification is a technique that helps you reduce risk by allocating your investment to various financial instruments, industries, and other categories. Diversification aims to maximize Returns By investing in different sectors or Industries that will react differently to the same market event. This way, you are not caught flat-footed or unawares by any shift or change in market conditions. Every investment manager or professional worth their salt will agree that, while diversification does not necessarily eliminate loss, it is crucial to see you reach your long-term financial goals while minimizing risk. Let's examine why that is true and how to diversify your investment portfolio.

A Brief Look at Risk

When investing, investors are usually confronted with two major types of risk. The first kind is called undiversifiable, systematic, or market risk. This kind of risk is the risk associated with every single company period, the common causes of this kind of risk at things like inflation rates, political instability, interest rates, war, and exchange rates. This kind of risk is not specific to any industry or company and cannot be eliminated or reduced by diversification. It's a risk that you must accept. The following kind of risk is called diversifiable risk; it is also known as unsystematic risk and is specific to an industry, a company, a market, a country, or an economy. Somebody can be eliminated via diversification. The most common sources are financial and business risk. As such, the idea behind diversification is to invest in various assets and asset classes such that your entire portfolio will not be affected by market events.

Reasons for Diversification

Reasons for diversification quickly become apparent when you take time to think about it, as you mean you have a portfolio that consists only of manufacturing companies. Suppose an issue affects the manufacturing industry negatively, such as the workers going on strike or a government ban or restriction. In that case, the share prices of manufacturing companies' stocks will drop, which means that your portfolio gets hit with quite a substantial loss. However, if you had invested a portion of your portfolio into another industry, say in the shipping or airline industry, then only a part of your portfolio would be affected. The value of the shares of companies in the shipping industry may increase because importation is likely to increase when manufacturing goes down. But you can diversify even further by investing in another industry that is entirely unrelated because anything that affects trade internationally could affect both stocks. Therefore, you will seek to diversify across more than just various companies or industries. The less the correlation among your assets, the better.

It is important to diversify among various asset classes. Asset classes such as stocks and bonds will not react similarly to an adverse market event. Thus, a portfolio with a combination of multiple asset classes will be less sensitive to market swings and possibly reduce the loss your portfolio will have experienced. Generally, equity and bond markets tend to move in opposite directions, so if you have a diversified portfolio across both markets, unpleasant movement in one asset class will be offset by the positive results you will gain in the other asset class. Finally, diversification should also include location. It would help to look for investment opportunities beyond your immediate geographical area. So, if you stay in the United States, for example, you should invest in assets outside the states, say in Europe or Asia.

Problems That Arise with Diversification

Diversification is, hands down, one of the best things that can happen to your investment portfolio, but it has its disadvantages too. A diversified portfolio is cumbersome, especially if you control multiple investments and holdings. Secondly, diversification affects your bottom line significantly. This is because investment vehicles come across differently. As such, buying and selling them can be expensive, from transaction fees to charges from your broker, and since higher rewards can only come with higher risk, you might end up limiting your results.

There are different kinds of diversification, and many synthetic investment products have been built to accommodate various risk tolerance levels of investors. However, many of these products are complicated to run and are meant to be used by something other than beginners or smaller investors. For a small-time investor with little substantial financial backing for hedging activities, bonds are the most popular way to diversify your portfolio.

Unfortunately, even the best analysis of a company, its stock, and your investment cannot guarantee that it will not be a losing investment, so diversification does not prevent losses; instead, it helps you reduce the impact of a loss or a negative market trend on your portfolio.

What is the Optimum Number of Stocks to Own?

Mathematical models and studies have shown that a well-maintained and diversified portfolio of between 25 and 30 stocks yields the most cost-effective level of reducing risk. Investing in securities will provide further diversification benefits but at a drastically reduced rate.

Diversification According to Asset Class

Investors and fund managers try to diversify their investments across different classes of assets and then ascertain the percentage of investment to be made in each category. The following asset classes can be used to diversify the investment portfolio.

- Shares or stocks of a publicly traded company.
- Corporate bonds and any other fixed-income debt instruments issued by the government.
- ETFs or exchange-traded funds comprise a variety of marketable securities belonging to different sectors or index commodities.
- Different real estate types include buildings, agricultural properties, livestock, land, and other natural resources like precious metals and minerals.
- Cash and other highly liquid short-term investments - treasury bills, certificates of deposit, money market instruments, and any other low-risk investments.

Further diversification is possible in various asset classes by selecting stocks across different industries that aren't related or by choosing supplies with varying degrees of market capitalization. When it comes to bonds, then investors can opt for bonds issued by the U.S. Treasury, municipal bonds, state bonds, investment-grade corporate bonds, and so on.

An investor can increase the degree of diversification by opting for foreign securities since they are unrelated to the securities issued by the investor's country of residence. For instance, the factors affecting the

U.S. economy might not be at play in a foreign country. So, the investor's foreign investments will be undisturbed even if the local stock market takes a blow.

The Retail Investor and Diversification

One of the significant constraints for sufficient diversification of a portfolio is the time and budget available to individual investors instead of traditional investors. This is one of the reasons why mutual funds are pretty enticing to retail investors. Mutual funds offer diversification of portfolios across multiple classes of assets. ETFs provide an opportunity for regular investors to access new markets like commodities. An investor with a $100,000 investment portfolio can easily invest across different types of investments across various ETFs without overlap.

Asset Allocation

Nothing Formula can provide the best way to allocate assets for every investor. However, most financial professionals know that the decision on the way to distribute your purchases is a critical one, which means that the journey of selecting the individual securities to invest in is secondary to how you allocate your assets to various asset classes such as stocks, bonds, and cash as well as their equivalent. Investors allocate their assets differently based on their objectives. An individual saving for a new car in the short-term, say, next year, might invest the cash savings in a very conservative mix of certificates of deposit, short-term Bonds, and cash.

Another individual saving for their retirement, which could be decades away, typically invests most of their money in an individual retirement account (IRA) in stocks; such a person has a longer time to withstand the market's short-term fluctuations. Risk appetite and tolerance also play a vital role in this. An individual not comfortable investing in stocks for a long time must invest cash in a more conservative asset class.

Asset Allocation Based on Age

Generally, stock investments are meant to be held for at least five years. Cash and money market accounts are much more appropriate for short-term objectives such as those less than a year—bonds for somewhere in between the short and long range. Financial advisors usually recommend subtracting the investors' age from 100 to determine what percentage of the Investment Portfolio should be in stocks. For instance, a 40-year-old should invest 60% of his portfolio in stocks. Other variants of this rule exist that advise the individual to subtract their age from 110 or 120 as life expectancy continues to grow. The idea, however, is that as individuals move closer to the retirement age, their portfolios should move towards a more conservative asset allocation to protect their accumulated assets.

Allocating assets via lifecycle funds

Asset-allocation mutual funds, which are also called lifecycle funds or target-date funds, attempt to provide investors with a portfolio structure that addresses their age, investment choices, and risk appetite asset classes in the appropriate proportions. However, this method has its critics, who point out that standardized solutions for allocating assets prove problematic as individual investors should possess unique solutions. An excellent example of this is the Vanguard target retirement 2030 fund. In 2018 the fund had a 12-year horizon until the shareholder is expected to reach their requirement age. As of 31st of January 2018, the front comprised 29% bonds and 71% stocks. As the years pass, the phone will slowly shift to a more conservative 50:50 mix, reflecting the investor's need to preserve the capital and take less risk. The fund will move even further to 67% bonds and 33% stocks in the following years.

Assets Allocation Vs. Diversification

While asset allocation and diversification are closely related, they are different. Asset allocation describes the percentage of a given portfolio held in various asset classes. Diver-satisfying and rebalancing, on the other hand, comprise allocating assets. So, asset allocation is more about the proportion of the portfolio appointed to various asset classes, and diversification is concerned with the investment itself that is invested in.

Rebalancing means changing the proportion of different assets within a portfolio. Asset allocation and fall out of alignment as the investors change their investment outlook and the economy changes. Rebalancing helps the distribution of assets within a portfolio to reflect the level of risk that the Investor is now comfortable with. Professional investors constantly seek to rebalance portfolios, while individuals rebalance less frequently.

Risk Tolerance

Risk tolerance measures the degree of uncertainty an investor will be willing to accept in exchange for higher or lesser gains. Investors with a higher level of risk tolerance will be ready to offer short-term losses in exchange for a potentially higher return. Risk tolerance also determines how much you must invest; a more extensive portfolio means you have more capital and can absorb more losses over time.

In conclusion, how you decide to allocate your acid and diversify your portfolio depends on you, your personal goals, and your age, size of portfolio, and risk tolerance. Most brokers have an education system, especially about their products, that explain how and why certain assets are allocated the way they are. If you want to diversify, ask questions from the company you are investing in, whether you are investing in mutual funds or Exchange- trust-Fund (ETF).

CHAPTER NINE

Setting Your Personal Investment Goals

Congratulations! You are almost ready to launch out. Before you do, however, you must answer some questions and build some investment goals for yourself, but how do you go about it? A quick online search for financial advice will deliver many resources and answers. It looks as though there is so much to choose from, and in this era of content marketing, every bank, broker, independent financial adviser, and their mother and looking to tell you what to do with your money.

Now, we have covered financial advisors in a separate chapter and, as such, will only go so deep into it here. The focus of this chapter is to help you build a personal investment plan that you will follow for the rest of your life. Whether you hire a professional financial advisor or not, an investment plan will help you decide your goals and objectives and spending habits that can get in the way of them.

Hire a Professional or Do it Yourself?

When it comes to investing, you can either hire the services of an investment adviser or create an investment plan by yourself. It is entirely up to you; choose accordingly. However, if you think you can get on by yourself, here are a couple of questions you must answer before coming to conclusions.

Do you like to read and learn about topics related to finance? Are you open to learning about different concepts like investment, taxes, loans, or personal finance? Knowledge is an indispensable resource, and you cannot do without it regarding investment. So, if you are naturally inclined towards learning about financial topics, your work will interest you. Your natural desire to learn will help you make better decisions and develop a sound investing strategy. Even if you don't like to read, before you start investing, it is quintessential that you do all the necessary homework. Start learning about personal finance and financial planning. Apart from all the information in this book, a wealth of knowledge is available online. After all, you are investing your hard-earned money, so learning about the different options is a good idea.

Review Your Current Financial Position. This is relatively easy if you are used to keeping track of your expenses, income, and savings. If not, you must start doing all this before considering investing. After all, you might end up overspending if you aren't sure of the funds available. You must be able to keep track of every single penny you spend. Once you do this, shift your focus toward your savings. Investing will help increase your income, but you must always have sufficient savings before investing. Start by learning to manage your finances, and only then attempt investing. If this seems too much for you, seek the help of an investment planner. How do you feel about making your own financial decisions? Have you planned for your retirement? Regardless of your earnings, you must permanently save for the future. Even if you have a

A comfortable and stable job that helps you rake in six- figures annually, you must concentrate on planning for your retirement. It is always better to save for a rainy day than be caught unawares. Also, take some time and think about whether you are comfortable handling large sums of your hard-earned money or not. If you don't feel confident about this, then hire a professional to do the necessary.

Will you handle the stock market volatility on your own? You will be your financial advisor if you want to do everything yourself. It would help to familiarize yourself with all the different investments in the stock market, learn about market trends and conditions, and develop self-control. You must know the right time to enter and exit the market. Apart from this, it would help if you learned to regulate your emotions while investing. Feelings of fear and greed can effectively burn a massive hole in your pocket if you aren't careful.

Managing your finances isn't scary; it only takes discipline, planning, saving, and investing. You can always manage your finances. You can start learning now even if you think you can't do this. After all, there is no time like now to learn about becoming a good investor and financial manager.

How to Set Investment Goals

Now, let's take some time to talk about setting investment goals. Lots of people have some idea of how they want their financial future to pan out like. Depending on where you are in life, you probably already have a dream of financial freedom. It could be sending your kids to college without needing to enter debt or being able to build your dream home. Many people, however, is that you don't know how to make your dreams become a reality, and so this section will detail how to make your financial future as accessible and secure as you can.

The first step to achieving your financial and Investment is to write them out. As simple as that may seem, it is a crucial first step to achieving your goal. The act of physically writing out your goals translates them from just a distant dream to a vision that you can see and begin to work on from now.

So briefly list out any short-term goals that you have. The keyword here is to be brief, talking about him in bullet points; a more detailed list will come later. You want to save for or purchase short-term goals within the next five years. An excellent example of a short-term plan could be replacing your car's tires or taking that vacation overseas that you've dreamed of. Next, you want to separate these goals into needs and wants. You must have a need, while a want is something you would like to have but is optional for you to have.

After that, make a brief list of your long-term goals. You want to achieve long-term goals in the next 5-years or even more. Whether to get married, have children, and your retirement can be classified as long-term goals. This is because these decisions will impact how you will live your life in the nearest future. For instance, if you are planning to get married, you should plan to move out of that two-bedroom apartment you are sharing with your roommate. Your long-term goals will be different based on your age. For those in their early 20s, things like marriage, kids, and a home fall under the classification of a long-term goal. But for another individual in his late thirties, his kids' college fund or retirement will probably be closer to a long-term plan. So, think and ask yourself what will make you happy or give you peace and fulfillment.

Once you've done that, it's time to investigate the details. List your goals in the order of most important to least important. With the most important at the top and the least important at the bottom, be as specific as possible instead of just writing your retirement as good at a particular number. Finally, attach a time frame to your goals. All reasonable goals have a time limit. For instance, if you are in your thirties and want to retire at 60, you have about 30 years to reach any retirement goal. So, do this for every plan that you have written down.

Here is an example for you to follow.

1. **Dream Home -** Build our $500,000 dream home within the next 20 years.

2. **College fund -** Save $125000 within the next 15 years for my kids' college tuition.

3. **Retirement -** I have $1000000 in my retirement fund by age 60.

Once to have a rough estimate of how much your future will cost you. It's time to take stock of how much you have. How much can you afford to set aside each month or year? When you know how much you can afford to set aside per time, it's time to build your investment portfolio. At this point, you need information, and luckily this book is full of it. Go back to Chapter 1 and start reading slowly, applying all the information in each chapter. By enquiring from brokers and financial advisers, you know how to invest your money and begin making moves.

I suggest that you sit down with a financial adviser, even if it's just for a limited time, for them to look over your plan and give you a few tips. Even if you're not planning to hire one for the long-term, and I don't think you should anyway, getting a second or even third Eye to look over your plan is for the best. So, look around for a financial advisor that is cheap and yet competent, and request a meeting with them to discuss your financial plan. You should revisit the project occasionally every few years to see where to revise.

Qualities of Investment Goals

As you set your financial and investment goals, here are a few things you want to remember. Your goals must be measurable: You must make sure that your goals are concise, clear, and definite. For example, saying that you will set a goal of saving $1000 per month is helpful because you can look at your finances and determine if you did for that month. On the other hand, a goal that says, "I will save more money each month," is useless because it does not hold you accountable and is not measurable. Your goals must be reasonable and rational: if your goal is to reach a million dollars in personal net worth by the age of 40, you have to use things like the time value of money formula to calculate whether or not the present rate at which you are saving will be sufficient, setting aside $5000 a year, as good as that may sound, will not get you there. Thus, you need to lower your expectations or increase the amount of money you're setting aside and choose an investment platform such as stocks to increase the amount you are potentially building up. Your goals must be compatible with your lifelong objectives: I cannot emphasize this enough because if you go through life with the mentality that money is the only thing that matters, you might end up rich but sad and miserable. Always remember that money exists to serve you — nothing more, nothing less. The entire purpose of having money or being financially free is to allow you to experience more happiness and utility. It makes no sense to sacrifice all your health to pursue money, for example, and then spend all your money to fix your health when you're older.

In conclusion, building a financial plan is not magic; all required is common sense, patience, and discipline. That mix is purely unbeatable.

CHAPTER TEN

Protecting Your Investment and Selling Stocks

Warren Buffet, one of the most successful investors, has a golden investment rule- never to lose money. It doesn't imply that you must sell your investments or holdings the minute they depreciate (this might be the best opportunity to purchase instead of the market). However, as a rule of thumb, stay put with your position up to the amount of loss you can withstand. All investors hope their investments are profitable, but you must first secure your capital in the long run to become a successful investor. As mentioned earlier, there are different steps you can follow to mitigate the risks while investing in the stock market. The strategies discussed in this section will help safeguard your portfolio.

Diversification

We've already treated this topic extensively in another chapter, so I will only go into some detail, but diversification is essential to protect your capital. The modern portfolio theory (MPT) believes in diversification as one of its cornerstones. A diversified portfolio is more likely to outperform one concentrated when viewed over a more extended period. According to several financial advisors, between 20 and 30 stocks eliminates almost all unsystematic risk.

It is investing in Assets that do not Correlate.

There are two types of risks that every investor will face: unsystematic risk and the opposite, systematic risk. Systematic risk is generally associated with an investment in any market. Systematic risk is the kind of risk that is inherent to every need, unfortunately. It is possible to mitigate its impact by incorporating assets that do not correlate to your portfolio or even going as far as to add asset classes that are not connected, such as currencies, real estate, commodities, as well as bonds, to the stocks that you probably already have in your investment portfolio. Assets that are not correlated react differently to market changes, sometimes even moving in opposite directions so that if an investment or an asset class goes down, the other is on its way up. This gives your portfolio a level of security and stability as compared to if your portfolio only contained stocks. Investing in assets that do not correlate helps you reduce the volatility of a portfolio. Unfortunately, using non-correlating assets does eliminate the higher and lower ends of the profit margins that could be seen if you were actively investing alone and produces returns that are more balanced, at least theoretically.

Put Options

From 1926 to 2009, the mutual fund index S&P 500 reduced in value for only 24 years out of the 84, or in other words, slightly above (25%) twenty-five percent of the period. In these situations, investors sometimes protect their gains by drawing some of their already-made profits. It may often turn out to be an intelligent choice, and often, it may not. This is because, in many instances, winning stocks may sometimes plateau for a bit before rising higher. In such cases as this, you don't want the store sold off, but at the same time, you want to cash in on some of the profit you have made, so how do you go about it?

There are several ways to do this, but the most used option is to purchase put options. A set option is like a bet on the line stock that will reduce the price. This differs from when you short the store; the put option allows you to sell the stock at a specific price at some point in the future, giving you some much-needed stability and confidence, irrespective of what the market goes through.

So, assuming you own a hundred share units of company X, the shares have risen in value by 80% in one year and are now being traded at $100 per share. As such, you are convinced that the stock price will increase in the distant future, but at the same time, you're concerned that the stock has risen far too rapidly and, as such, will likely fall in the short term. To protect your gains, you will purchase one put option of the company X, with an expiry date of 6 months ahead, sold for a strike price of $105, and could even be slightly more than that. The cost of purchasing this option will then be$6 per share or $600, which gives you the right and ability to sell 100 share units of company X at $105 sometimes before it expires in 6 months.

Should the share price fall to, say, $90, the price of buying the option will increase by quite a significant margin, and you can then sell off the opportunity to make a profit and eliminate the fall in the stock price. Investors that want to be protected in the long term can also decide to buy Long-Term Equity Anticipation Securities (LEAPS), which usually come with much more extended periods, sometimes up to 3 years.

Stop Losses

A stop-loss order can help protect your investment from the falling prices of shares. There are various kinds of stop-losses that you can use. A hard stop will trigger a sale on a stock once its price reaches a particular value. For instance, if you purchase company X's Shares at $10 for a share, using an order for a hard stop set at $9, then the stock automatically is sold off If the price hits $9. Trailing stops, however, is quite different in that it tends to move alongside the stock price and could be pre-set to either percentage or dollars. Maintaining the example above, as you mean, you set the trailing stop to 10%. Should the stock increase by $2, the set trailing stop order moves from $10.80

to $9. Should the stock price later fall till it gets to $10.50, with the hard stop set at $9, you still retain ownership of the stock. However, somebody will have sold off the share for $10.80 with a trailing finish. Whatever follows this, however, determines which will have been more profitable. A trailing stop loss would have been more advantageous if the stock price had dropped from $10.50 to $9. However, if the price had later moved to $15, you would have been better off with a hard stop loss.

Critics of the complex and trailing stops claim that it makes temporary losses permanent, while the proponents of the orders believe that it helps protect you from markets that change rapidly. I will advise, however, that somebody must plan well, and any stop you use must be very well prepared.

Dividends

Investing in dividend stocks is a strange way to safeguard your portfolio. Historically, rewards are responsible for a significant portion of the total return. In many instances, a store brings even the total amount.

One of the proven methods for providing returns that are higher than average is by owning stable firms that pay out dividends. Also added to the income invested, studies have shown that the companies which pay their investors more significant rewards tend to increase their earnings at a faster rate when compared to those that do. More rapid growth will often lead to share prices rising higher, which will, in turn, generate even more capital gains.

But how exactly does this help in protecting the portfolio? It does this by basically increasing the overall return. As the prices of stocks fall, the cushion provided by dividends is considered necessary for investors that are averse to risks and will usually result in low volatility.

So, while providing a cushion when the market is in a downturn, dividends are also excellent protection against the effects of inflation. Via investments made in blue-chip companies, companies that have pricing power and pay dividends, you give your portfolio the kind of protection that other investments with fixed income cannot match, except for TIPS or (Treasury Inflation-Protected Securities). What's more, if you do invest in companies that have had their dividends increase consecutively for the past 25 years, called "dividend aristocrats," you can say for sure that such companies will increase the amount they pay out each year while the pay-out of bonds remains roughly at the same level. As you get closer to retirement, you want to prepare to prevent increased inflation from destroying your money's purchasing power.

Notes Protected by the Principal

Investors concerned with maintaining their principal should look at notes protected by the principal and have equity participation rights. They are like bonds in that they are securities with fixed incomes that return the principal investments to the investor if it is held to maturity. However, the significant difference is that equity participation is simultaneous with the guaranteed principal.

For example, if you considered buying $1,000 worth of principal-protected notes fixed to the S&P 500. This note will mature in 5 years, and the party issuing them will then purchase zero-coupon bonds, which will grow roughly the same period that the letters will have discounted to Face value. As such, the bonds wouldn't receive any interest until maturity, when you can redeem them at their face value. In the example above, the $1,000 that is in zero-coupon bonds can be bought for

$800, and as such, the $200 left can be invested into call options of the S&P 500.

These bonds will then mature and depend on the participation rate; the profits will be distributed when they reach maturity. Assuming the index increased by 20% over the stipulated period and the participation rate is 90%, you'd get your original $1,000 investment plus a profit of $180. You are essentially letting go of $20 in profits in exchange for a guarantee that your principal is guaranteed. However, if the index did lose 20% over the five years, you'd still receive the original $1,000 you invested. If you had invested directly into the index, your investment would have lost $200.

Investors that tolerate few risks will find principal-protected notes quite essential. However, before you decide to invest in it, you should take time to determine how strong the bank is offering a guarantee on your principal, as well as the notes' underlying investment of the letters and the fees associated with buying them.

How to Sell Your Stocks

Here are a couple of ways that you could use to sell a stock, with some additional background on how to decide to sell.

Order an Order

The easiest way to sell any stock is via a sell order. The primary type of orders related to sales are market orders (which involves selling the stock instantly at the market price), as well as limit order (which set a minimum accepted sales price), as well as a stop order (that initiates the sale of the stock once it reaches a sufficiently low price)

Using an App

Beginner traders are fond of trying to play the market because many investment applications do not require a commission to sell.

Using a Financial Advisor

If you purchased your stock from a financial advisor, you could also decide to sell off the stocks similarly. A financial advisor usually takes 24 hours to execute a request to sell. You should, however, note that if you make this decision, you have to talk to the advisor directly or send a written appeal. As was stated in Investopedia, "Financial institutions will not readily accept a request via email or voicemail as somebody can miss them quickly or even third parties can manipulate.

A Magic Selling Number: 16.5

This digit has nothing to do with the share price, calendar date, or secret code from a smoke-filled room on Wall Street. Instead, it pertains to something known as a GAAP forward multiple. Let's break that jargon: GAAP is "generally accepted accounting principles," a financial standard that public companies use.

If you take the earnings per share of a company as determined by GAAP and multiply it by 16.5, you now have a target price for your sale. So, if Carlozo Motors has earnings per share of $10, your target sell price will be $160.50. Why the number 16.5? This is based on a 40-year average for equities and has been in the ballpark of 16.5 since the late 1800s.

Market Timing and its Untimeliness

Someone must answer besides knowing how somebody can sell a stock. How do you decide when to sell a stock? Well, there are different answers to this question. Let us look at the various solutions starting with a technique not usually favored while selling stocks - market timing.

The concept of market timing is based on the theory that an investor can successfully buy and sell stocks by predicting the future movements of a market. This is based on guesswork, starting with the mortgage interest rates and then betting on the ideal time to sell and the price. This technique isn't precise. Most stock market experts believe this technique is a wager. Even if the world of investing is chock-a-block with numbers, there is no specific calculation to determine the ideal time to enter or exit a position. This might pay off if you don't mind taking a gamble. After all, you are effectively guessing the ideal time to get in and out of the market.

It is always better to set a specific dollar value whenever you want to sell instead of hoping to get the time right. It is like a sell order, the only difference being that this isn't a legally binding agreement. For instance, if the dollar value for sale is

$30, then if a $25 stock reaches the said price, it is time to sell. It is a better way to deal than relying on guesswork.

Putting Everything Together

Considering the various methods you can use to buy or sell a stock, entry barriers are low in the investment world. Suppose you are concerned about how to sell a stock or when you can adopt the "*sitting and waiting*" approach. The buy-and-hold strategy is one that successful investors such as Warren Buffet have used in the past.

Afterword

We've come a long way, and I want to believe that. You know all you need about stocks and the stock market to begin making money from it. We've covered quite a bit of things that are important for you to know. Somebody created for beginners who wanted to invest in the stock market had the desire to invest in the stock market but had no idea how to go about it, and I want to believe that right now, you know enough to begin investing in the stock market.

Let's quickly recap everything we've covered in this book and how you can and should apply it to profit from the stock market.

We started by looking at investments and what they are, and why you should think about creating a financial and investment plan for yourself.

We also talked extensively about risk tolerance and Investment Portfolios. In the introductory chapter, I introduced the concept of high-risk, high-reward, and low-risk low-reward. You should consider this concept as your stock market investment journey progresses.

Next, I explained the stock market and how you can make money from trading in the stock market. Then we considered a few of the greatest investors to show you what was possible via stock market trading. We also looked at the wonders of compound interest and how it can seemingly magically provide you with a fortune if you invest long enough.

In this book, I explained in depth everything that you need to know to be successful on the stock market, starting from why you should invest in the stock market to the basic fundamental knowledge you will need to understand the time to understand common terminologies that you will find as you go on things like price-to-earnings ratios, Sales ratio, book value and many more.

I also touched on practical things you will need to know to invest in the stock market, such as brokers, especially online brokers, the minimum amount you will need to open an account, and how to deal with commissions and fees, which is extremely important as it has the potential to wipe out your account if you're not careful for example in 1% commission can potentially take 25% of your Investment Portfolio if you are running an active investing strategy.

Next, we covered financial advisors as part of the strategies you should put in place to manage your money; I explained the different kinds of advice we have, such as a financial planner and investment advisor, and the fact that advisors are expensive and not the best idea for a beginner or small-time investor.

From there, I explained the alternatives to financial advisers, such as robot advisors. Finally, I ended that chapter by discussing mutual funds and why you should pay attention to them. Mutual funds offer a safe, low-risk option for a short time and beginner investors to invest and build their investment portfolio. Why diversify your portfolio and eliminate the chances of your investment portfolio losing value over the long term?

We then took an honest view of how some of the greatest investors ever made remarkable gains. We examined their trading strategies and philosophies, and in the following few chapters, we discussed the plan in-depth and the reasoning behind them. The last three branches of the book are all about index investing and why you should consider making it a part of an Investment Portfolio by looking at diversification and asset allocation to safeguard your investments. Then we ended with a look at how to preserve your investment and how to sell the stocks.

As I promised earlier, investing in the stock market is not a get-rich-quick scheme; it is a platform to generate profits via long-term investing, and that is the best way to make sustainable profits for the long term. I hope you build your investment portfolio and a future of true financial freedom by reading this book. It may be worthwhile going back through the book and taking notes to be confident that you are following the advice given. I hope you find investing in the stock market as profitable and enjoyable as I have.

Thank You

You could have picked from hundreds of other books, but you bought mine, and I appreciate it. Thank you so much for purchasing my book.

Not that you enjoyed (I hope) my book, can I ask you for a tiny favor? Can you please post a review on the platform? You posting a review is the best way to support the work of independent authors like me.

Your feedback will help me keep writing the books that will help you get the desired results. It means a lot to me to hear from you.

I am happy for anyone to reach out to me for help, comments, collaboration ideas, or feedback at brian@brianscottfitzgerald.com

Visit my author page with this link or Scan this QR code

https://www.amazon.com/author/brianscottfitzgerald.

www.ingramcontent.com/pod-product-compliance
Lightning Source LLC
LaVergne TN
LVHW100307210926
848480LV00003B/1050
9798349534454